THE DESIRED ARTICLE

A Concise Look At Style

By
J L Disley

Published by ZANI

The Desired Article: A Concise Look At Style
© Words - 2022 by Jason Disley (J.L Disley). Electronic compilation/ paperback edition copyright © 2022 by Jason Disley / ZANI

All rights reserved. No part of this book may be reproduced, scanned, or transmitted in any form or by any means, electronic or mechanical, including photocopying, recording, or any information storage and retrieval system, without permission in writing from the publisher. Please do not participate in or encourage piracy of copyrighted materials in violation of the author's rights. Purchase only authorised eBook editions.

While the author has made every effort to provide accurate information at the time of publication, neither the publisher nor the author assumes any responsibility for errors, or for changes that occur after publication. Further, the publisher does not have any control over and does not assume any responsibility for author or third-party websites or their contents. How the eBook displays on a given reader is beyond the publisher's control.

For information contact:
info@zani.co.uk

Contents

Foreword	v
Introduction	vii
Rolling With The OCBD Shirt	1
From Snappy Sportswear To A Style Culture Staple The Tennis/Polo Shirt, And Branding	5
Cooking The Creases: STA-PREST	10
The Harrington Jacket, And The Roll Call Of The Cool	13
Don't Pull The Wool Over My Eyes: Merino Is Mighty Fine	17
Turtlenecks Through The Years, A History Of Rebellion And Style	21
In The Navy– The Pea Coat/Reefer Jacket And Bridge Coat	26
The Winter Hero: From The Chesterfield To The Crombie	30
Suits And International Style – What Makes The Cut	34
Just The Tonik – Mohair, And Dormeuil	39
Silk Blades – And A Short Sharp History Of The Neck Tie	43
A Link To The Past – A Brief History About Cufflinks	50
That Touch Of Class – The Pocket Square	56
Tootal Scarves – A History Of Elegance And Modernism	61

Don't Be Stingy – Tell Me About The Pork Pie Hat	65
The Accessory That Fits The Bill – The Money Clip	71
The Khaki Experiment And The Chino Cinch	75
The White T-shirt – A Canvas Of Expression And Style	81
From Wabash To Hickory, And A Bit Of Acid Jazz Style	85
Chambray – The Versatile Comfort Of The Blue Collar, And Work Wear Style	89
The Classic Enduring Style Of The Breton Top	93
Bermuda Shorts – A Legacy That Has Not Been Lost	97
Throwing In The Towel With Style – From 007 To French Terry	101
A Tailored History Of Madras – Check It Out	106
Seersucker – The Milk And Sugar Of Cool Fabric	113
From The Correspondent – An Article About Brogues, Imperials And Spectators	117
From Loafing Around To An Iconic Style: A History Of The Loafer	122
When It Rains, It Pours – The Return Of The Mac	127
Falling For Flannel – That Autumnal Fabric, And Bags Of Style!	132
Weaving A Tale Of Tweed	138
Corduroy: A Short History On The Fabric That Can Draw A Line Between – And Fashion	144
The Origins Of Paisley, Ancient Babylon, And Indulgence	148
Conclusion	153
Afterword	155
Acknowledgements	157

Foreword

I have a memory of me aged around 10/11, laying out my outfit on my bed for the day ahead. The memory of actual clothes involved is now lost in time, but the fact I was piecing a look together at that relatively young age, I think shows how important clothes have always been to me.

'Fussy' is the way I would describe it. I won't pretend that I knew then, the exact reason why I would wear 'that,' but not 'that,' but I just knew how important it was to feel right in whatever I put on. And let's have it right, I did it for me. No one else. I didn't dress to impress anyone else. This was all about how right it felt on me. Even having the wrong colour socks on, could ruin my day.

And now 50 years later as I approach the age of 60, that feeling is still there and as fierce as ever. To paraphrase the legendary Liverpool manager Bill Shankly, clothes aren't life and death, they are much more important than that.

So, it was with some delight to hear of this book from the prolific pen of Jason Disley. Within it, he details the history of many of the garms that have played such a special part of my life and I suspect if you are reading this, yours too. What follows, is a detailed and extensive collection of articles on everything from Polo Shirts to Paisley, from Mohair to Madras and they fascinate and educate in equal measure.

J L Disley

Simply put, if you love your clobber, then this is the book for you. Your bookshelf will be underdressed without it, and we can't have that can we?

Mark Baxter
Spring 2022

Introduction

It may seem like Groundhog Day sometimes, especially when you get dressed every morning. Apart from when there is a special occasion, which is when you will make even more conscious decisions on what to wear. Whether it be for work, rest or play we are all conditioned from birth to dress appropriately – according to season, climate or the activity we are about embark on. But, although we do these things, many of us do not want to look like everyone else. Naturally we like variety. It could be colour, texture, pattern or shape. We want to feel comfortable, and more often than not, some of us, want to look, not only properly attired, but also look our very best. If you have bought this book. No doubt you will be interested in clothes and ultimately a history of those stylish items or fabrics that you are attracted to. Hence the title The Desired Article.

Throughout the last year or so I have been writing regular articles about "articles" of clothing, fabric and style. After some comments and suggestions from writers such as Rick Blackman, and Matteo Sedazzari, it was agreed that these articles should be brought together in a book, so as to serve as a potted history of some of the most well known items of clothing, and fabrics that still appeal to many of us today. Being a man whose main interest in clothes is of course those items I like to wear – the book is more orientated towards gentlemen's attire. So naturally, there will be many things that I will not have addressed. As I say it is a potted history of what I know, and understand. There are items of clothing that years after they were first created, are still hugely popular today, and often will appear either in the high street stores and online shops of clothing retailers. These articles of clothing that are reproduced with only slight variation year on year are often related to what has become termed as style. The cliché that fashion comes and goes, and that style is timeless is somewhat true. People, myself included are often inspired by outfits worn by celebrities, whether it be a musician, a movie star, a person in a magazine, or a person that has built their own brand via multi media. Fashion and style *is* big business, there is no denying that. But, as lifestyles change, so what we consume is gradually changing. Leisure activities are changing, and society's needs are being moulded by the environment that we have created. As a consequence, some of the things in this book, may begin to look quaint or old fashioned. But in truth, as we look at the history behind things such as say a Tweed jacket, or a particular raincoat, we see their practicality, the innovations in producing the garment. The workmanship involved and the hard-working lengths that have been gone through to clothe an ever-growing population. Vintage fashion and styles often get an increase in popularity due to the cyclical nature of fashion, and perhaps the idea that you can not reinvent the wheel. Trousers work, because they do their job. A Jacket does too. So, it is natural that the success of all these items is what I have endeavoured to show. The Desired Article is a success story about just some of these things that many of us see as stylish. It is a brief, and not exhaustive history book. It is meant as an introduction to style, but is not a style guide. It is up to you reader, what you want to wear, and how you want to dress. I just thought it would be nice to record some of

The Desired Article

the history about those items that have endured through generations, and are still relevant to those that consider what and why something is stylish. No doubt in years to come, new styles will appear, but right now we have a template and centuries of successful styles to draw upon and appreciate. So, here in this book are the articles, those about items I myself have desired, and have worn, and then the other pieces I have written about such as fabrics like Merino wool, and their history, so that I hope you too reader, may be interested in elements of style history.

Jason Disley December 2021

Rolling With The OCBD Shirt

When, you read about the youth culture known as Mods, and the many other cultural styles, that past decades have seen – such as Skinheads, Suedeheads, and those that like to adopt a Preppy or Ivy style. You will sometimes read the acronym "OCBD shirt". This stands for Oxford Cloth Button Down. It is quite possibly the most popular style of shirt in the last century, in that it is stylish, and can be worn both casually and formally. Here I look into the history of the style. It's origins, and the popularity of this versatile and seemingly timeless garment.

History has it that John Brooks in 1896 saw the Oxford shirt's true potential.

Firstly, as the name implies, the OCBD is made out of Oxford cloth. The fabric is made of a distinctive weave which, though similar to a plain canvas weave, uses several yarns woven together instead of individually. This tends to produce a breathable cotton garment with a textured finish.

Although many points about the shirt have changed with time, two enduring traits linger. The shirt is made out of the Oxford cloth, and it features the button-down collar. The second, and most important trait, is a genuine OCBD should have a distinctive collar roll.

This is where, due to precisely this collar design, a popular garment evolved. It managed to look smart without the need for a tie, yet was quite capable of taking one when required. John Brooks just happened to be the grandson of the founder of Brooks Brothers. It was whilst on a trip to England, and watching a Polo match, that he noticed that the players' collars – which were large and tended to flap, as dictated by the current fashion, and the game's regulations – had been fastened down to their shirts to stop this flapping around during the time they were playing, which if they had not been, would have made the sport all the more dangerous by possibly impairing their vision, whilst cantering around on horseback.

Impressed by the elegant arch, or 'collar roll', the buttons induced, he (John Brooks) promptly took the idea, and America's once upon a time, most important menswear retailer made the button-down shirt its own. In fact, the button-down was to become one of the core garments of the preppy, Ivy League style – which is, arguably the most influential look in modern-day menswear history.

To say that over the next half century or so men of influence took to the OCBD is without doubt an understatement. Clark Gable, who had a 44-inch chest and a 32-inch waist in his prime, was generally unable to wear ready-to-wear clothing except for the Brooks Brothers button-down shirt, which he promptly did, day in, and day out. John F. Kennedy wore it too, helping to make him the first style icon with his finger on both the fashion and nuclear buttons.

Musicians, Chet Baker and Miles Davis – both outfitted for fame in Charlie Davidson's The Andover Shop, the mecca of preppy – both took to button-downs like Charlie Parker to the Alto Sax. Miles would wear it in his own way: with a knotted handkerchief tucked into the open collar. Gianni Agnelli, of the family behind Fiat, wore his with the collar buttons undone, (a look that feels wrong to me – but, when adopting the Italian notion of sprezzatura is totally acceptable.) Other stars became associated with the style. Paul Newman for example, and it is these high-profile celebrities that have inspired shirt style collections ever since. When you look at the history of Modernists, and later the Mods, you see that their inspiration for true style came from the wish to look sharp and rich. They wanted to be like their style icons, and naturally adopted certain garments they saw either in the cinema, in magazines or on the covers of records. Probably one of the most famous examples of a OCBD is the one worn by the aforementioned Miles Davis. The cover of his album Milestones shows him sat relaxed on a mid twentieth century stool with a orange/tan background. He is wearing a green OCBD which stands out beautifully. The detail is there, the afore mentioned all important collar roll. The casual comfort of it, whilst still looking like Miles means business. It looks effortlessly cool, and of course natural. A powerful image for any, young jazz enthusiast, who wanted to buy into that particular style.

Many companies take inspiration from the original Brooks

Brothers polo shirt, and the button-down shirt can be found everywhere today. It is a style that will not go away. It is in affect timeless because of its functionality. I could list so many different companies that produce these style shirts, but in truth the number of companies that get the collars right, is not many. More niche companies such as Charles Caine, Capirari and DNA Groove produce shirts with all the necessary details, and there are countless other independent shirt makers that will do shirts that tick all the boxes. But, these days – many of the big guns have tried to move with the times, or have bowed to the pressure of cutting production costs, and have got it wrong. Say Gant for example. Their more recent shirts often have a smaller collar, so lack that all important, and attractive collar roll. Ben Sherman – arguably the first British firm to adopt the Button Down has done the same. Their more recent shirts seem to have small collars. Sure, the buttons are there. But only for show. The functionality seemingly lost. Mods want authenticity, as do members of other subcultures. It is in all the details, and if your OCBD doesn't have the correct details, it is considered inferior. The cloth has to be right; the roll has to be right, basically the shirt has to be right. How else can you feel as cool as those that have inspired your style?

From Snappy Sportswear To A Style Culture Staple. The Tennis/Polo Shirt, And Branding

The earliest known roots of polo reach back as far as 6th century BC, the modern form of the horseback sport can be traced back to the 19th Century in India. British military men stationed in Manipur, a state in Northeast India, adopted polo from the indigenous Indians, and brought it back to the U.K. where it became synonymous with wealth, royalty, and the upper-classes.

In addition to jodhpur pants and full-length riding boots, the original polo uniforms included a long-sleeved cotton shirt, similar to a dress shirt. To stop their shirt collars from flapping in the wind while they rallied around the polo field, players would secure them down with pins or buttons. Inspired by this was John E. Brooks of the successful Brooks Brothers firm, who noticed the players' improvisational collar solution while visiting England in the late 1800s. Upon his return to the U.S. Brooks introduced button-down collars onto all of his dress shirts, a feature that has become commonplace in modern-day shirting. Brooks Brothers introduced the first mass-marketed 'polo shirt' by debuting the 'The Original Button-Down Polo Shirt' in 1896.

However, what is commonly known as the polo shirt we know today was born from a completely different sport—tennis.

Like polo, tennis 'whites' in the early 1900s featured a long-sleeved button-down shirt. Looking to improve the practicality of this design was French tennis star, Jean René Lacoste. Nicknamed 'le Crocodile' due to his agility and "snappy" shot power. Lacoste won seven Grand Slam titles, making him one of the most sensational sportsmen of his era.

While most tennis stars wore a button-down shirt and tie, Lacoste went against the grain and introduced his own short sleeved, three button shirt, made from a lightweight, breathable pique cotton that improved freedom of movement on the court. Proud of his reptilian nickname, Lacoste had a crocodile embroidered onto the left breast of his tennis shirt, a piece that surprised spectators as he smashed his way to consecutive U.S.

Open wins in 1926 and 1927. The first of its kind, Lacoste's tennis shirt was the blueprint for what is considered the modern-day polo shirt.

After retiring in the early 1930s, Lacoste was approached by the owner of a leading French knitwear manufacturer, André Gillier, who proposed that the two came together to sell reproductions of Lacoste's knitted tennis shirt, complete with the infamous embroidered crocodile. In 1933, the pair founded La Chemise Lacoste. Now known simply as 'Lacoste', the brand is widely regarded as the first brand to produce clothes with clear, visible branding on the outside of the garment.

La Chemise Lacoste was not the first brand to popularise the knitted polo shirt. Independent makers and brands like John Smedley had already capitalized in on René Lacoste's revolutionary design. But it was Lacoste's formidable reputation and playful crocodile branding that made his tennis shirt so desirable. Understandably this popularity gave rise to other sportsmen being attracted to the idea of creating their own versions and ultimately brands. One such was the English tennis star Fred Perry.

In the 1940s, Fred Perry was approached by an ex-Austrian football player, Tibby Wegner, who is credited with having invented the first sweatband. Wegner and Perry worked together to launch the sweatband as the first product in the Fred Perry range of clothes.

Fred Perry was the Roger Federer of his day with three Wimbledon titles under his belt and, like the stars of today, this approach to put his name to a range of sports products must have been not only very flattering but a shrewd investment at the time.

After the launch of the simple sweat band, the Fred Perry brand was born. That humble idea for the logo, the laurel wreath, was incredibly important in its popular appeal. It is now one of the most recognised logos worldwide, and is still very popular – especially amongst youth groups and subcultures. The Mods identified with the logo. When headlines, and the infamous speech by Margate magistrate Dr. George Simpson's sentencing speech after clashes during a weekend in 1964 accused the Mods (and rockers) in the Dock he said,

> "It is not likely that the air of this town has ever been polluted by the hordes of hooligans, male and female, such as we have seen this weekend. These long haired, mentally unstable, petty little hoodlums. These Sawdust Caesars, who can only find courage like rats hunting in packs, came to Margate with the avowed intent on interfering with the life and properties of its inhabitants"

This term "Sawdust Caesars" practically made the laurel wreath design on the Fred Perry tennis/polo shirt a badge of honour and an identifier. After all the history of the laurel wreath was associated with champions, and leaders since biblical times, and is indeed associated with images of Julius Caesar the famous Roman Emperor.

So, although both the laurel wreath design from Fred Perry and the Tennis shirt had been popular before 1964, it's appeal to a subculture was well and truly cemented, and was adopted by those that identified with the evolving Mods, who were a far cry from the Modernists of the 1950s, who wouldn't be seen in such casual attire, unless participating in a sport.

Today the Polo shirt is widely available on the High Street, thanks to its wearability. It has become a fashion staple for those less formal times. The two or three button opening and collar allow for the wearer to button up for a smarter look.

Since the mid 20th century, the innovation of wearing sportswear as daywear saw students, and political leaders alike, often adopting the tennis/polo shirt. (See US President JF Kennedy, and images of college and university campuses).

Designer Ralph Lauren is famous for his Ivy League, and Preppy inspired designs. He often teams such a garment beneath a sports jacket. Essentially "dressing up" a casual style. His "Polo" range reinforcing the transition of a simple Tennis shirt into the term Polo shirt. Which is quite different from the original idea of the Brooks Brother's Polo Shirt.

The polo shirt, like the simple t shirt are here to stay it seems, because of their style and comfort. All thanks to a French Tennis player who was a snappy dresser.

Cooking The Creases: STA-PREST

From inventing the blue jean in 1873, Levi's has always been an innovator when it comes to clothing, always functional, and suited to both work and play. So, it's no surprise that in the 1960s they found a way to put a permanent crease into trousers. A process that meant, no ironing was required and was quite literally desirable by all. Let's face it. Ironing used to be a real chore, and, so very time consuming!

The process was called STA-PREST, and it really was an immediate hit, and consequently it became an iconic look of that era. But, how did it all start?

Koret of California, a women's garment manufacturer, first came up with the idea, patenting a system for permanent pleats in 1961. A finished product was coated with a chemical resin and a catalyst. Creases were made with a steam press and then the garment was baked in an oven at 300° Fahrenheit, triggering the catalyst that made the resin bond with the fabric. The result? The now famous, permanent crease.

Levi Strauss &Co. Sportswear Merchandise Manager Mel Bacharach decided to experiment with the permanent pleat idea, and came up with his own process for garments, which he subsequently named STA-PREST clothing.

Curing ovens were installed at the company's Knoxville, Tennessee, factory. Apparently, a few managers were heard to mutter, "If this doesn't work, we're going to be baking a lot of bread in Knoxville." Thankfully the process was a success, and expanding waistlines, were not an immediate hazard.

The first Sta-Prest garments were produced in 1963. They were trousers made from 100 percent cotton twill and sateen. These high-end slacks were made to be sold during the 1964 season. Although they were at once popular, it was soon discovered that all-cotton clothing could not withstand the curing process. Eventually, all products had to be made with synthetic fabrics, or blends of synthetic and natural fabrics (usually consisting of a 65/35 blend), to be able to withstand the temperatures needed to create the permanent crease.

"Never Needs Ironing" was the company's slogan. It was cleverly aimed at both retailers, and of course, the buying public. Some sales reps actually took off their Sta-Prest trousers and threw them into portable washers and dryers to demonstrate how successful the permanent crease was. Certainly, this will have helped sales, but undoubtedly caused some uncomfortable encounters, with the people they were selling to.

In the late 1990s the Sta-Prest name was revived for a sharp-looking collection of tops and bottoms. It is still revived from time to time, as it is an iconic style, that really has never fully disappeared. With today's more innovative fabrics, Levi's and other brands do still make clothes that are made to be wrinkle free. The permanent crease isn't as prevalent as it used to be, but for some, it is still a requirement to look razor sharp.

Initially in the mid 60s Sta-Prest were thought to be perfect for workers who needed a durable-but-fresh-looking pair of pants for daily wear, they quickly became the go-to pants for Mods, the youth subculture that coalesced around fashion, music and scooters in the mid-'60s London. The Mods were, in many ways, the progenitors of today's youth culture, and their legacy of making style a testament to personal expression has become the prevailing attitude of modern life. I have stated in previous articles, that Mods, were inspired by the Ivy League Style from America, and indeed it wasn't long before Sta-Prest were being worn on campuses, this could have also been one of the reasons why Levi's has been especially popular with the Mod scene. I think when you look at original images and advertisements for Sta-Prest, you can see why they are still a sought-after garment. In fact, original Sta-Prest, really are collector's items today, and are still popular amongst some subcultures and style tribes.

The Harrington Jacket, And The Roll Call Of The Cool

When, it comes to the Harrington Jacket, I feel a sense of pride. I am from the North West of England. I was born in Salford and was brought up in Greater Manchester. For those that don't know – the versatile and simply smart casual jacket originated in the form as we know it, in Manchester, the metropolis that was at the centre of England's textile industry, and had been, since the industrial revolution.

I mean, if you look at the Twentieth century, and if you had to pick out one British-designed garment that has transcended numerous decades, and had earned its right as a favourite amongst sportsmen and Hollywood greats alike, and infiltrated its way into the wardrobe of fringe subcultures, the Harrington jacket, simply stands taller than any other.

It is impossible not to talk about the Harrington jacket and not begin by paying homage to its originators of the style of this classic and extremely wearable garment, Baracuta.

Baracuta was founded in 1937 by James and Isaac Miller in Manchester, they "designed the G9 (The G stands for Golf) when they set out to create a functional rainproof jacket for the English modern working man,"

The company is inextricably linked to the Harrington jacket. In the same year it was founded, the brand released the iconic G9, which then only became known as the 'Harrington' after the rise of US TV soap opera Peyton Place, in which a character – Rodney Harrington played by Ryan O'Neal – would often wear the style.

John Simons, the purveyor of American classic styles is considered to be the most influential man in Britain with regards to Ivy Style and quality garments, plays a part in this tale of the Harrington jacket. As aforementioned there was a character in Peyton Place played by Ryan O'Neal called Rodney Harrington. Legend has it, that Simons would hand write cards to go in the window next to the garments on show. He would write for example "The Rodney Harrington Jacket" when displaying a Baracuta G9 in his shop window. After doing this a few times the writing of the name was shortened simply to "The Harrington"

The Harrington jacket's original purpose was to be worn in the great outdoors. Traditionally, its shell is a water-repellent poly-cotton blend with an umbrella-inspired vent on the back to aid the run-off of rainwater so one's trousers don't get wet. There are also two slanted flap pockets with concealed buttons and an elasticated waistband and cuffs to keep you dry. The collar is a double-button, stand-up, Mandarin-esque collar which can be snapped shut to stop the incoming rain. There is also a central fastening zip. Overall, it's incredibly lightweight, yet its signature element is the tartan lining of Lord Lovat, a British commando and chief of the Fraser Clan, who gave Baracuta's founding brothers permission to use his family's colours in 1938. Since then, this has remained an unchanged feature on Baracuta Harrington's. Why? Because according to Paul Harvey, a designer at Baracuta, "firstly it must be simple and not follow fashion. Secondly, proportions and balance are vital to such a simple design. Thirdly, it has to feel right. The simplicity of the jacket asks nothing of you and that means you feel totally comfortable wearing it."

It's simple design and look has been worn by many that have become style icons. Movie and music legends alike have been known to wear Harrington jackets. It's no surprise that stylists from many different backgrounds have gravitated towards wearing a G9, or more recently Harrington jackets that have been manufactured by other manufacturers. For it is testament to this garment that it has been copied widely, as its influence is such that it is the embodiment of cool. When you see James Dean, Elvis Presley, Frank Sinatra and the King of Cool Steve McQueen wearing a Baracuta, it makes you want to buy into that coolness. When you see the Mods, Skinheads, Britpoppers and indie artists looking cool in Harrington's you acknowledge that sense of style for an easy to wear, sharp and understated look.

I myself have several Harrington's. From cheaper ones to

one's that are much more expensive. They are in various different fabrics. I have three Baracuta's. One is in the traditional water repellent fabric, one that is in Chambray cotton, and another is a rare lightweight summer one, that is in red polyester and has a mesh Fraser tartan lining. I also have a Harrington style jacket by Two Stoned, that has the legend "The Two Stoned Rodney Harrington Style Jacket" on the label, and had been purposefully aged to look vintage and has several "Northern Soul" patches on it. I have a vintage US college version of a Harrington made by Haband of Patterson, New Jersey which is more like the Baracuta G4, and a black Leather G9 style Harrington I wear in the, autumn and winter that is made by Charles Caine.

Harrington's are functional, comfortable and timeless. The functionality is what appeals to most men, and the knowledge that when you slip one on, you instantly join that roll call of the cool. Of course – Harrington's look great on women also. As when the fairer sex chooses to wear masculine clothing to successfully subvert style norms, so they choose items that men have looked up to and admired. In affect reaffirming that they too can join that roll call, and show that they also like the functionality, comfort and design that has a history that is broad, long and full of cultural identity.

Harrington's are here to stay for it is the jacket that is made for both work and play.

Don't Pull The Wool Over My Eyes: Merino Is Mighty Fine

When it comes to knitwear that is comfortable, warm and not bulky. You can't go wrong with an extra fine Merino. Popular for its fine lightweight quality it has been a fashion staple for quite some time.

So, where does Merino wool come from? Not surprisingly, it comes from Merino Sheep.

Merino sheep were developed in South Western Spain, and were highly prized because of their fine wool. The wool helped significantly, in the economic growth of Spain during the 15th and 16th centuries. In 1797, the first Merino sheep, derived from the famous Royal Merino Flocks of Spain, were introduced into Australia. Although these sheep had already evolved a fine fibre, further selective breeding by Australian farmers soon produced the authentic Australian Merino with its even finer wool. Which is the wool we are much more familiar with today.

Australian Merino wool has played, and still continues to play, a major role in international fashion. Being a highly resilient wool, it has predominantly been used in utilitarian garments, particularly military uniforms and work wear. But wool's big fashion break came in the decade following the First World War, when Coco Chanel reinvented the fashion rules and produced a dress from fine wool jersey. Since then, wool has continued to be used in fashion.

The end of the Second World War heralded another fashion revolution called 'The New Look'. Launched by the House of Christian Dior, the style used excessive amounts of wool fabric in designs as a backlash against the rations and shortages of the war years.

In 1954, young designer Yves Saint Laurent won first and third prizes in the dress category of the International Wool Secretariat competition in Paris while a young Karl Lagerfeld won first prize in the coat category. Accepting their respective fashion design prizes, from a judging panel which included Hubert de Givenchy and Pierre Balmain, fashion history was made.

Over the years, classic and much-loved looks have benefitted from Merino wool's qualities. From the little black dress, to the V-neck jumper, to fine tailored suits, Merino wool has timeless appeal. Today, fashion designers and wool farmers across the world continue to work alongside the best textile manufacturers to produce quality Merino wool apparel and connect consumers with its natural benefits.

But what has it got to do with the British subculture known as Mod? Well, one of the leading quality knitwear manufacturers in the world is the brand, John Smedley. It is a brand that is admired greatly for its products and were seen as great additions to a Mod's wardrobe. After all -the silhouette of a fine gauge piece of knitwear, was always going to be favourable to a style conscious Mod, who wanted to look slick and lean.

The John Smedley story begins during the infancy of the industrial revolution at their factory in Lea Mills, Derbyshire, where you can still find them.

In 1784 the factory started life producing simple muslin fabric and spinning cotton, and in 1825 they had moved into producing much more complex garments using one of the first ever fully fashioned knitting machines and creating the original "Long Johns".

By 1914 they began exporting to the far reaches of the globe and over time, had established themselves as one of Britain's most famous clothing brands.

By the 1950's and 60's they had become the brand of choice for many famous faces, including Marilyn Monroe, Audrey Hepburn and the Beatles amongst many others, and by 1980 they had established themselves as the go-to knitwear brand for British designers such as Dame Vivienne Westwood and Sir Paul Smith.

They are also particularly proud to have "Made in Great Britain" on the tag of every garment they created.

By 1963, Mods, as many will know, were no longer the cult group of young people that hung about in Soho, as referenced in Colin Macinnes novel Absolute Beginners, the subculture that had been referred to as Modernists had evolved and become a nationwide subculture. Mods met in all night cafés and danced in Jazz clubs – where the Mod style evolved further. Although the slim fitting suits looked the part, they weren't always practical and, in some cases, not always affordable.

A much more casual look was created, although it was still very smart. It didn't require a tie – the iconic Parka Jacket was often worn over a long-sleeved Polo shirt, with its collar buttoned up, and tailored Trousers or Jeans. The early Mods didn't particularly like wearing logos on their clothes as they thought that off-the-peg clothes represented an off-the-peg lifestyle which they were trying to move away from, so they chose not to wear Polo shirts that had a logo. Apart from, as the scene evolved and diluted itself even more, brands like Fred Perry, whose logo was small, and had eventually become acceptable, but that is another story, as has been revealed in an earlier article in this book.

All this attention to detail, and an eye for classic design meant that John Smedley became a firm favourite among the subculture. With stars and icons wearing the brand, it was natural young people wanted to buy into that. So, consequently Mods have maintained a healthy relationship with John Smedley, that has lasted even to this day.

There are plenty of companies who have taken the influence of Mod styling and have produced Merino wool items of their own – you can find some lovely Merino cycling jerseys; alongside every style of knitted garment, you can think of. Although John Smedley the essentially British company, is still the original, and regarded the best. It has to be noted that Merino is a fabric of choice because of its association with the knitwear favoured by the stylish. It is the elitism of the brand John Smedley, and the quality of its Merino and sea island cotton products, that the relationship with Mods has endured.

Turtlenecks Through The Years, A History Of Rebellion And Style

Turtlenecks have been a staple item of western wardrobes for many a year now.

While they seem to be predominantly worn by women, everyone gets in on the turtleneck game once winter comes around.

It can be said that Turtlenecks have been symbols of strength, rebellion, style, and modesty throughout history. I often jump at any chance I can get to wear one. Why? You may ask – Well, wearing a turtleneck makes me feel stylish and – (ahem) cool. The garment feels at once both understated, yet stylish. Many style icons, from pop stars to film stars, and society's rebels have worn them. These associations make so much sense once put into context with this popular item's history.

The turtleneck is said to have originated among the fishermen of the Aran Islands; a collection of rocky islands located just off the western coast of Ireland. The position of the Aran islands in the North Atlantic Ocean made seafaring a decidedly frigid affair, but those courageous, and dedicated Aran fishermen weren't going to allow a little cold to keep them from sailing. Instead, they bundled up and created a number of styles we still know today.

The most successful of these creations was undoubtedly the turtleneck. Those first turtlenecks worn by the Aran fisherman were designed for purely utilitarian purposes, and as such were woven from heavy, dense cloth that could keep a fisherman warm amid a sea squall. But the most important—and identifiable—feature was the signature rolled neck, which is also what gave it the term "roll neck sweater", when the style carried over to Britain.

It was also in Britain—and soon, the United States as well—that the turtleneck cast off its exclusive associations with sailing and was adopted for a wide variety of outdoor activities and sports. In an age before performance fabrics, the coverage that was provided by a turtleneck sweater made it an invaluable article of clothing for newly popular activities like cycling, hiking and – polo.

But just as the turtleneck had found new wearers beyond its original cast of Irish fishermen, the turtleneck craze soon spread to those who weren't doing any physical activity at all. Thanks to the example of dashing 1930's Hollywood movie stars like Errol

Flynn, turtlenecks began to be worn with suits and men's sport coats. These turtlenecks had little in common with what those Aran fishermen originally wore: in order to slip under a jacket, these turtlenecks were woven from lighter, finer fabrics such as merino wool or cotton. This was the moment in the history of the turtleneck when the garment first began to resemble the version most commonly seen today.

But the turtleneck wasn't done with the sea yet. During WWII, German U-boats posed a great danger to Allied shipping. To combat this threat and keep the vital supply line between the United States and Great Britain open, the Allies waged what became known as The Battle of the North Atlantic. Thousands of American merchant marines were deployed to the same waters trawled by the Aran fisherman a century before, and relied on hearty, military-issue turtlenecks to keep warm as they guarded convoys and swept for mines.

When the war ended, ex-servicemen attending college on the GI Bill continued to wear some of the same clothing they'd been issued in the war on college campuses, including chinos, pea coats, and turtlenecks. Before too long, turtlenecks became a common sight amid college quads, and were adopted by yet another group—the beatniks.

This loose collection of artists, jazz musicians and writers like Jack Kerouac made the turtleneck part of their daily uniform, often pairing it with chinos, desert boots, and the occasional beret. Before long, the turtleneck had become downright counter-cultural.

But once again, Hollywood came knocking. The turtleneck saw a resurgence on-screen and off in the 1960s, as it was worn by Audrey Hepburn, Steve McQueen and other luminaries of the silver screen.

What's most striking about the history of the turtleneck is the different types of people and places where it has been worn. From salty Irish fisherman to movie stars, from the naval battles of WWII to Greenwich Village jazz clubs, the turtleneck has never found a time or place where it couldn't warm a few necks and look good doing it.

Its connection to rebellious, and less conservative style only grew during the 70s. Feminist activists like Dorothy Pitman Hughes and Gloria Steinem, as well as groups such as the Black Panthers donned these distinctive tops. Turtlenecks supplied a style that was both uniform and unique at the same time. Their subversive nature had become the equivalent of say the rebellious nature of a black leather jacket, which had become synonymous with rebellious youths in the 1950s.

After an eventful decade as a staple of the resistance, the turtleneck in the US had a bit of a resting period in the 1980s. This decade saw the garment become "uncool" and swiftly moved into the background as just another basic. This lasted into the 90s, when it began to make a resurgence. In the UK however, perhaps because of the nation's climate. Turtlenecks were still seen regularly. Especially among those who were into certain subcultures, styles of music, and were part of popular club wear.

In the workplace there was the beginning of a more relaxed and informal look beginning to appear in offices. Especially in firms associated with modern computerised technology.

These individuals meant business but didn't actually want to be in business—and the turtleneck created a costume that was both anti-establishment, yet not distracting from the work that they were doing.

For example, the turtleneck's reputations of anti-establishment, and being a bit nerdy, married in the form of Steve Jobs's daily outfit. Although it wasn't a 'deliberate choice' on Jobs' part to wear an item of clothing that holds a contentious, rebellious history, it does definitely fit into the narrative that turtlenecks are worn and represent those who do not conform to the strict traditions and like to colour outside the lines. It could be said that Jobs was actually drawn to the article of clothing for the same reasons activists were during the 70s. These individuals meant business but didn't actually want to be in business—and the turtleneck created a costume that was both anti-establishment, yet not distracting from the work that they were doing.

Maybe that's why I can pull on a turtle neck or a roll neck and still feel smart and ready for action. Just like style icon Steve McQueen in his famous blue Roll neck and his brown herringbone jacket in Bullitt. Or the quintessential secret agent that has become associated with the 60s during the Cold War, as popularised in The Man From U. N. C. L. E. By David McCallum as Illya Kuryakin. Or, at least not forgetting the iconic look of John, Paul, George and Ringo – who as The Beatles – popularised the longevity of the style of a simple black turtleneck and made the beatnik style fully acceptable.

In The Navy— The Pea Coat/Reefer Jacket And Bridge Coat

When you do some research on the Pea coat you find some different origins. Probably, like with many things that people independently of each other, they have had the same idea or at least quite similar ideas to solve a problem. In the case of the Pea coat, the problem to solve was how to protect a sailor/person from wind and rain. Before the invention of rubberised fabrics and the types of waterproofing we are used to today, the options were limited to what was available. As we have seen, the popularity of wool clothing goes back a long way, and it's practical application for many garments is very clear. The Pea coat was no exception.

Pea coats (or pea jackets) were originally worn by sailors in the European and later American Navy. They have been used for well over 300 years, and have achieved an almost legendary status.

The word pea most likely stems from the Dutch or West Frisian word pijjekker. The pij referred to the coarse kind of twilled blue fabric with a nap on one side, and jekker is associated with jacket. The fabric goes back to the 16th century.

At that time, the Dutch were very big in world trade, and had a very strong naval component, as did of course Britain. In the British language, the Pea coat was often called a Reefer.

In America, the earliest mention of the Pea coat is during the 1720s. The reason it seems, that the coat became known as a Reefer Jacket, is because a "Reefer" was referring to the sailors who would climb the rigging of a ship and would wear such a coat that was reasonably short, it's length just sitting below the hips, it also had a slight flair to the skirt allowing for ease of movement. Officers, who would not be seen doing such tasks had longer coats, coats which of course helped keep them warmer – these were often referred to as Bridge Coats.

Originally, the collar on the Pea coat was designed, to serve sailors exposed to the inevitable cold and open winds at sea. The collar can be worn up, almost as a half hood, without impairing the sailors sight. Although not applicable to most who wear a Pea coat now regarding the open winds at sea, but with winter coming it could be a great contingency plan responding to a winter cold snap when without key accessories. Turning the collar up, would at least keep you both a bit more sheltered and warmer.

The other standardised feature to the coat is the double-breasted front. It gives a real feeling of integrity and class to the coat, even though the far side buttons will never be used and are there for show. (Although I do suppose, if you lost a button, you would have spares to choose from!)

Aside from these two main features, there is often the inclusion of two slanted pockets reasonably high up on the jacket for the purpose of keeping the sailor's hands warm and dry when not carrying out important tasks.

The material: This double-breasted coat was typically made from navy-coloured heavy wool. Historically, until the 1970s, in the US Navy, Pea coats were made from 30oz (approx. 850g) dark blue wool, more often than not – heavy Melton cloth. Modern pea coats are made from 22–32oz (620–910g) wool in a variety of colours. The heavy Melton wool is durable, and tight. The latter makes it a great insulator to keep out cold and wind, and even some sea spray or rain.

While enjoying steady popularity among civilians since their introduction, Pea Coats saw a sharp increase in demand during the 1960s, as military surplus fashion became chic in the midst of the anti-war movement protesting against conflicts such as the one that was happening in Vietnam. As second-hand military attire became a key element in Hippie fashion, pea coats became the preferred winter coat for the flower children. While green Army jackets fell in-and-out of style in later decades due to an intimate association with the anti-war movement. The Pea coat drifted into mainstream tastes and has never really left.

In part, the Pea coat's staying power is a result of never being merely a counterculture symbol. From hip college students to high society, the Pea coat was ubiquitous. The jacket was just as prevalent with hippies and the anti-establishment as it was with the establishment.

Robert Redford, made the Pea coat a staple of his look. His style in *Three Days of the Condor*, was anchored by a black Pea coat, and remains iconic to this day and helped establish the jacket's hard masculine edge. Many other celebrities from Music and Film have worn a Pea coat, firmly establishing it as a staple of a stylish wardrobe.

I remember seeing a photo of Keith Richards of the Rolling Stones that was taken in 1965 by Pierre Fournier where he is looking typically Mod in jeans, Cuban heeled boots, a short jacket, and then a Pea coat resting on his shoulders, all topped with a little cap, and thinking, wow that's a cool look, and since then I have always liked the style of such a coat.

It's style has changed very little over the years, and these days you can see many coats use the style of the Pea coat as a template. It can come in different fabrics, including Leather, and has spawned many variations thanks to its double breasted fastening, and large collar.

It really is a smart and practical style, that has really made itself one of the most popular coat styles we have today. The reason for this is because it's aforementioned double breasted fastening, has echoes of smart tailoring, and when a Pea coat is worn during the second half of the year, it not only makes the wearer warm, but looks extremely smart also. As with so many popular items of clothing, there is not only its original purpose, but its ability to please the eye and last for a long time. A decent Pea coat can last for years, and really never goes out of fashion.

The Winter Hero: From The Chesterfield To The Crombie

The hero of Winter dressing will always be the overcoat. Warm, luxurious and thoroughly practical, a beautifully tailored overcoat gives any wearer an air of stature and style.

What is an overcoat? Not to be confused with a topcoat, an overcoat is a tailored coat which is traditionally knee-length or longer. Made from a warm, heavyweight cloth, such as wool or a wool/cashmere blend, they can be either single or double-breasted. They usually feature a single rear vent.

The overcoat has been a key part of a gentleman's wardrobe since it was invented in the late 18th century. They were often worn as formalwear to represent the wearer's social status or as part of their uniform, both professional and military. The style of the overcoat hasn't changed much since then, apart from some very subtle changes made according to whatever the trends are at the time.

It was, for instance, very fashionable during the Regency period to wear form-fitting clothes, subsequently, the overcoats of the time were worn closely fitted to the body; usually double-breasted in style, with waist seams and a flared skirt. As the popularity of the overcoat grew and it became available to the working classes, the silhouette became looser, so as to accommodate their lifestyle.

There are several styles of overcoat, all variations similar but slightly different.

The first I draw your attention to is the Chesterfield. It became fashionable in the 19th century. It is said that the Earl of Chesterfield had this style of coat made by his tailor. But whether he is actually the creator of the Chesterfield is debatable, purely because of the similarity of it to other coats. The coat is available both in single breasted and double breasted. Quite often made in a woollen cloth with a herringbone pattern. It usually has a fly front and is knee length or slightly longer. Some will have slanted flap pockets like a hacking jacket, including possibly a ticket pocket, and a welt pocket on the chest.

Another style is one that is not mentioned a great deal these days, and owes its look and use to the Military. Called the British Warm, this coat is made of thick Melton wool like the Pea Coat. It has epaulettes and is double breasted. Usually two flap pockets, and no ticket pocket. There is also a variant of this coat that usually comes in Cashmere. This one is usually longer and is similar in style to the Trench Coats that officers wore in WW1.

Next, we come to another variant, and that is one called The Covert. This coat is quite similar in style to The Chesterfield. It is slim fitting, sits above the knee, and although has features in common with the Chesterfield, such as a fly front, the same pockets, such as the three flap pockets, and a chest welt pocket, and the inclusion of a velvet collar. It is the twill fabric, and the fact it can be worn all year round makes it popular. Originally it was a hunting or riding coat. On the inside of it, there is usually another large pocket level with the thigh, which was usually used for provisions or ammunition. So quite possibly that's the reason why so many old style "Gangsters" used to like wearing them.

Lastly, we come to the one style that has become well known especially in the UK, and that is The Crombie. Although in regards of style it has been around since the end of the 18th century. The brand Crombie didn't produce coats of it own until as recently 1985. Crombie were essentially a fabric manufacturer, and their woollen mill was established in 1805 by John Crombie in Aberdeen, where it was able to produce high quality woollen fabric. John saw that it was good business to sell these fabrics they made directly to tailors, as well as other merchants.

By the mid 19th century its fabrics had become not only fashionable on Savile Row, but we're being exported on a global scale. During the American Civil War, for example, Crombie's booming business was able to provide the grey cloth used to uniform the Confederate Army, all while markets in Canada, Japan and Russia were getting well established, and all by the turn of the 20th century.

Crombie produced hundreds of miles of cloth for blankets and uniforms during both world wars. Between them the Crombie family sold the business to Salts – a company named in honour of the entrepreneurial Yorkshireman Titus Salt, who built Saltaire and popularised alpaca. In 1958 Salts was subsumed into the Illingworth Morris empire, and later inherited by Pamela Mason, the ex-wife of James Mason. During the 1980s the group was acquired by Alan Lewis, the Conservative Party's vice-chairman for business.

Under Lewis, Crombie's emphasis shifted: in 1985 the first Crombie-branded collection of coats, and other wares were produced, and in the early 1990s production moved to Yorkshire. The collection of Crombie branded clothes is still going strong – garments include plenty of City and skinhead-friendly covert style coats, and what we would term The English Town overcoat. Which is tailored from thick woollen cloth.

There are different variations of this coat, and many other brands often do their own versions. Next for instance do a Crombie style coat called an Epsom. But, where it differs from the Crombie, is that it doesn't have the welt pocket on the left chest. Any well-dressed Mod, Skinhead or Suedehead, would be frustrated by this missing detail, I am sure. But for the chap who wants a coat to go to the races or work in the city. It isn't a bad coat. All of these coats, do their job. They serve their purpose and keep their wearer clean and dry. So, whether you are a Russian Spy, a Gangster, a Banker or a racing enthusiast, or just an average Joe. There is always an overcoat worth getting, and they always look smart, and are perfect for when things get a bit chilly.

Suits And International Style – What Makes The Cut

It is said every bespoke tailor has its own signature tailoring style, which has been developed by years and years of – experience, knowledge, and their artistic creativity.

Over the years suit styles have developed. Nowadays you will see a lot of suits that mix the different features and styles. However, traditionally there are three suit styles that are the template. Those styles are British, American and Italian.

The Desired Article

Now, I don't profess to know everything about tailoring. I am not a tailor, nor am I man of means that regularly goes bespoke. But I find the topic of style, taste and what I see as aesthetically pleasing and fascinating, to the point – where I want to know more. So, here in this short article I focus on the differences between the British, American and Italian suits. My research not only informing myself, but also passing on that information to those of you (excuse the pun) that are suitably interested.

The British suit style finds its origins in Savile Row. Savile Row's place in the formal history of suiting was cemented in the mid-19th century, when the Prince of Wales the future George IV, ordered a tailless smoking jacket, a relatively informal jacket style, made out of the fabrics traditional for a tailcoat. The Prince's new style, was eventually named as a dinner jacket, and it soon developed into a trend that revolutionised British fashion, and helped to introduce some more casual styles into the strictly regulated canon of English dress wear.

The vision of the prince regent, together with the creative mind of a skilled tailor, sir Henry Poole, slowly changed what was considered formal wear amongst an extremely traditional high class. The dinner jacket, and, of course, the whole new suit style they created, had a set of unique characteristics that persisted through time, and were not surprisingly passed from each subsequent generation to the next, and were soon seen as what was to become "British style", and the actual start of a tradition, that has remained ever since.

The British suit is emphasised by structured shoulders, a stiff canvas and low shoulder lines or Gorge as it is known. This line, helped to give the jacket a very sophisticated look. The fit is tailored to be close to the body, with close fitting sleeves ending with surgeon's cuffs and a high armhole. The jacket can either be single-breasted or double breasted, with usually two vents and a ticket pocket. The pants have a high waist and can have up to three pleats.

When it comes to the American style, it has to be noted the rise in popularity of these suits came in the 1920s and was led by those that would be considered as Ivy Leaguers. (Those that were part of the American ruling class and were educated in those elite colleges that were called Ivy League: Harvard, Yale, Dartmouth, Columbia, Princeton, Pennsylvania, Brown and Cornell.)

At the turn of the 20th century, a distinctly American suit style appeared among the world's fashions. This was known as the sack suit. Modelled after a French coat from the 1840s, the sack suit was loosely-fitted, and gave its wearer a much softer silhouette compared to the much more structured and military style of British tailoring. Manufacturers, like Brooks Brothers, were looking for low-cost garments to produce in large quantities, garments that allowed for a much more industrialised production. Because the sack style was meant to look baggy, it was already a one-size-fits-all product. Consequently, less variation meant it was less expensive.

In its original form this suit is perhaps considered the least stylish. Its distinguished characteristics are a single (hook) vent in the back, a higher armhole, straight lines, flap pockets and natural (almost not padded, and in some cases not padded at all) shoulders, therefore, the afore mentioned softer silhouette. These suits were quite loose fitting. The looser cut in these suits was helpful, when the wearer had to spend countless hours in them. The coat was single breasted with two or three buttons. (Sometimes the lapel was allowed to have a roll that allowed the top button to hide under the lapel, so the wearer could have the choice of wearing it as a two button jacket, instead of a three button jacket. This became known as a three roll two jacket.) The sleeves were also a bit looser and would usually feature three buttons only. The main characteristics of the trousers were that they were not pleated, and they were cut quite full, compared to European tailoring.

Brioni is widely credited as the innovator of the "Italian" style. They introduced their style to the world in 1952, at the first fashion show to feature a male model as its focal point. Especially in America it got famous because of the 1953 movie 'Roman Holiday', in which Gregory Peck wore Brioni suits. The "new" Italian style quickly won popularity over the American suit and the British suit. In fact, the importance of cinema and Italian style cannot be ignored when it comes to modern style. In Britain for example, it was the style of Italian tailoring that captured the imagination of the new generation of young men that thanks to movies such as Roman Holiday, they felt they could emulate a more continental look, rather than the standard, and quite sombre tailoring the previous generation wore. To these young men it was thoroughly modern, and that is what they became known as: Modernists. Modernists, in fact took inspiration from wherever they could find it, and appropriated it for themselves, hence Modernists also taking inspiration from the American Ivy Style, and what their Jazz musician heroes wore. But, getting back to the Italian suit.

The Italian suit style is a modern, trendy cut – and is characteristically very slim. Italians were not comfortable in the structured British suit. The majority of British tailoring also used fabrics that was suitable for its cooler and damper climate. They were too heavy to be worn comfortably in the much warmer, and dryer Italian climate. The Italian's preferring to use much lighter cloth. Therefore, the feel of the suit is much lighter, and more comfortable. The jacket is considerably less structured compared to the British one, and as a result of that, the cloth follows the natural curves of the wearer. The jacket is notably a little bit shorter, shoulders are padded, and the jacket has a V-shape. Pockets are flapless and the shoulder/gorge lines are higher. The jackets originally did not have any vents but today two vents are common in Italian suits. The pants have a tapered waist and are tighter on the hips.

Over time these basic elements in the three original styles have blurred. Fashion will dictate what elements are popular, but the fundamental cuts have remained, allowing for individuals to cherry pick what they want when they choose their suits if going to a tailor, or by choosing what they like on offer from where they decide to purchase such items of clothing.

It is fascinating how little suits have changed in the last century. Sadly as "leisure wear" becomes more prevalent in society, so the wearing of what were known as lounge suits is becoming less prevalent. However, when society is given more opportunity in the future to mingle, maybe the penchant to dress up when going out may become popular again and the importance of sartorial matters will also rise.

Just The Tonik – Mohair, And Dormeuil

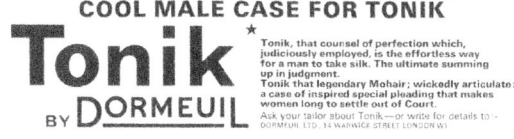

I heard the Charlie Rich song – Mohair Sam the other day, and it made me smile, and groove a little. It also inspired me, and made me want to write about Mohair, and about a brand that was in the mid twentieth century, was the leading brand for suits using Mohair fabric, and is still today held in very high regard.

Mohair, quite rightly, is associated with great style, and is quite clearly something that is still appreciated, although it is perhaps more associated with the fashion and style of past generations. The excellence of such fabric is still in use today by many, if not all tailors, and high end brands.

Mohair comes from the Angora Goat – which originated in Turkey. The word mohair comes from the Turkish word "muyha", which translates to "the best selected fleece". Unlike other natural fibres, mohair handles dye colours with ease, and is one of the reasons why it became so popular. Who doesn't love a suit in an unusual colour or one with a particularly rich tone?

Angora goats were introduced to the U.S in the mid 1800s as a gift from Turkey.

During the second world war the U.S were so fearful of a wool shortage due to their military uniforms being made entirely of wool, that they decided to combat this by blending mohair with wool. The subsequent use of Mohair in the military would soon act as a stepping stone into an ever evolving fashion hungry world.

But why Mohair?

Mohair is still one of the best fibres around, due to its durability, breathability, lustre and its natural elasticity.

Mohair is taken from the underside of the Angora Goat, and comes in three grades: kid, young adult and adult. The latter being the coarser of the three – which is why many tailors source their mohair from the young.

One of the subcultures that propelled the mohair movement into the eye of the public, was of course the iconic Mod subculture

(Yes –I know –that term again.) The mid 50s gave birth to the London-based rakish youths with a taste for modern jazz. These modernists were inspired by the style of musicians and movie stars alike. Continental style, and American style inspired these young style conscious people, and as a consequence they would search out garments, styles and fabrics that would allow them to push the envelope and create looks that either looked like their inspirations or were tweaked versions that would be subtly different thanks to added details, so their garments were practically unique.

Their main armament was the mohair suit, and in particular, Dormeuil tonik mohair. (House of Dormeuil) actually coined the term 'tonik' in 1958, and now it's used to describe any suit with a sheen.

Dormeuil whose history, from its origins to present day, can be tracked down through famous, innovative creations, starting from 1922, when their mill launched Sportex, the first cloth to have a woven selvedge.

The cloth was designed to keep warmth without restricting movement and became a must for European outdoors sportsmen. Thanks to the sweeping success of Sportex the company was able to expand further, moving its headquarters to Regent Street in London's West End, which is the world's epicentre of textile retail.

From their new West End home, Dormeuil released Frilex in 1936. The pure wool fabric was created with a very aerated, plain weave, and a special construction that made it extremely fresh to wear and quick to dry. Dormeuil had once again exceeded the expectations of sportsmen across the world, including professional tennis players.

By the time we reach the 1950s, collaborating with Paris's haute couture, in 1957, the Dormeuil Mill launched Tonik. The cloth was entirely woven in England, and the pure three-ply mohair weft, combined with special processing and finish, gave the fabric a very distinctive sheen.

The fashion industry was experiencing radical changes, such as the introduction of the ready-to-wear, and the fast paced evolution of fashion during the 60s, saw a growth in markets as the buying power amongst the post war generation had grown, and subsequently tastes for desirable items for that generation expanded. The Dormeuil family was not intimidated by this, and responded well to such changes in demand, and introduced its very first ready-to-wear collection.

In England as Tonik became all the rage, so many stylists would wear the wonderful fabric. As processes developed, so the whole two tone effect of the tonik fabrics became a noticeable attraction for those that bought into the super sharp style, and so it has remained ever since. As decades went by, two tone tonics were adopted by some other subcultures. Such as The Suede heads, for example. The sheen of a good tonic Mohair suit has always attracted customers. Although it may go in and out of the spotlight from time to time as tastes change. There is always those who look back and still want unusual fabric, in amazing colours, and if you can afford it, you know you are going to have quality, and a statement piece. A Mohair suit is flashy, and gets you noticed. It's iconic. You only have to look at the Mohair suits that the likes of Sean Connery, Michael Caine, and other movie stars have worn on screen, to see how cool and stylish a good Mohair suit is. You feel uplifted and sharp when wearing them. It seems a good Mohair suit is more than a fabric. It really is a real tonic, in a world that often needs brightening up.

Silk Blades — And A Short Sharp History Of The Neck Tie

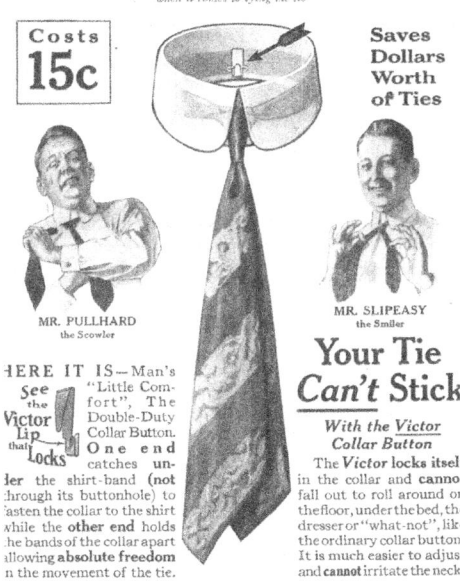

There was a time when no outfit was complete without a tie. It adds class and sophistication to ones look. But, have you ever asked yourself why we wear ties?

They don't keep us warm or dry and they certainly don't add comfort. So why do some people love wearing them?

I have taken it upon myself, to find out more, for I am actually one of those that likes wearing a tie, whereas it seems the majority of us don't, unless it's a particularly formal occasion where it is usually expected.

Neckties, bowties, scarves, and cravats — neckwear is without doubt one of the most fascinating elements of men's apparel. With just the change of a tie, a man can alter his persona from 1920s gangster to 1950s rebel to a 1960s ad man. Just at a first glance through 20th century men's tie history, you may think a tie is simply a tie, and a tie is a tie, and that's it. But with a keen eye on the subtle differences between colours, patterns, fabrics, and size, much more can be revealed.

During the 30 year war in France. King Louis XIII hired Croatian mercenaries, who wore a piece of cloth around their neck as part of their uniform. While these early neckties did serve a function (tying the top of their jackets closed), they also had quite a decorative effect – a look that King Louis liked a lot. In fact, he liked it so much that he made these ties a mandatory accessory for Royal gatherings, and – to honour the Croatian soldiers – he gave this clothing piece the name "La Cravate" – the name for necktie in French.

The early cravats of the 17th century have little resemblance to today's necktie, yet it was a style that stayed popular throughout Europe for over 200 years. The tie as we know it today did not actually appear until the 1920s, and since then, it has undergone many (often subtle) changes.

During the early twentieth century, and most of the 1920s, men's neckwear came in such a variety of colours, shapes and styles, that it could be considered the best era for men's ties. It was also the start of the modern necktie as we know it today.

Previously, the bow tie was very popular for day wear with popular patterns of horizontal stripes, checks and polka dots in light pinks, purples, greys, and greens. Neckties, too, were full of colour from the "club" or "regimental" striped ties – which started in Europe to the gold toned paisley prints that were especially popular in the USA. All-over prints of stripes, checks, and diamond patterns also reigned supreme in Europe during this time.

Neckties were thin — about 2 and 3/8 inches — and made of very fine silk. The quality of the man was often judged by the quality of his silk tie.

The knitted tie also appeared in the 1920s, usually with a squared end. This style is one that has come and gone over the years. Probably the most popular era for such a tie was during the 1960s.

Getting back to the 1920s, as styles developed, so things began to change. By the thirties, scarf ties and bow ties were quickly becoming less fashionable, leaving only the silk necktie to dominate. Multiple colours of horizontal stripes, checks, paisley, large dots, pin dots and Art Deco motifs clashed with men's shirts. It was wild and colourful, and made great statements about the wearer.

Hand-painted Art Deco designs started in the 1920s, but really found a place in the 1930s. Famous artists would hand paint ties as a way of bringing art into everyday life. Necktie widths grew wider (about 3.5 inches) and shorter to go with the wider suit lapels and the oversized shirt collars of the '30s.

When war time struck, so did restrictions on men's ties. Silk was in short supply, so rayon and wool knit ties were the thing to buy. Shortly after WWII, men's ties took a radical shift in style. No longer confined by fabric rationing, men's ties got wide — very wide — and short to the point of ending above the belt line, which was already high on the waist. These have eventually become known as Swing ties, as the popular music of the 40s was the jazz style called swing. Hand painted ties were still popular, and the way geometric, curly lines, monograms, and Art Deco style patterns were painted in bright colours of blue, red, gold and brown. Animals, plants, flowers, birds, western, and tropical printed themes were everywhere. Hand painted ties were actually often themed around the wearer's hobbies and interests, such as – painting, fishing, sailing or hunting. Hand painted ties needed a large canvas, so naturally neckties grew in size, and became 4.5 to 5 inches wide. They were given nicknames such as "scrambled egg ties" because of the mix of muddled circles and darts the patterns created. Stars such as Bob Hope would often wear these styles of ties, and because they were wider, they also became known as "Belly Warmers."

The painted tie continued to be popular in the early '50s. The designs became more abstract, cubist, modern, and artistic than the '40s designs. It was less about the hobby and more about a play on colour, shape and stand-out designs. These days, they are highly collectible now.

Wide ties gradually narrowed again by the mid '50s to a "normal" width of about 3 and 1/8 inches. Bow ties, too, slimmed down and straightened out into the skinny ribbon tie. The conservative look was in with businessmen in grey flannel suits, Oxford shirts, and a graduated striped tie. Neutral ties with light patterns were also common. Young kids were wearing knit ties on college campuses, a trend last seen in the '20s. It wasn't the pattern or colour that was big news in the early '50s, but the material. Among traditional silk and wool, men could now find the latest synthetic Dracon knit, which offered a noticeable texture on solid colours. Other textured materials like coarse silk and shantung were trending in the mid '50s in America.

Ties kept on getting narrower as we move into the 1960s, when the ultra-thin 2 inch skinny tie came in vogue to go with narrower silhouetted suits. Solid colours and striped designs were preferred in most '50s business attire, while mod art designs reigned in the '60s. Both traditionally pointed neckties and square end ties had their place. Pink, purple, yellow, and aqua colours were seen with large geometric shapes, wide stripes, and square dots.

In 1964 the silk ascot returned in solid colours, figure prints, and Mod patterns. They were worn tucked into unbuttoned shirts. The puffed ascot look was very chic and quite big for the time. That is until 1968, when the wide tie returned bigger than ever. Most ties were 3 and ¾ inch but they could go up to 5 inches with big knots that needed a wide-cut collar such as the spread to accommodate them. This enormously wide tie was called the Kipper tie, created by Michael Fish. The Kipper tie was huge and came in bold colours, small feminine prints, and psychedelic swirls. It was meant to stand out and give the wearer true personality. The Kipper tie was literally the biggest thing to happen to men's neckwear in decades.

In formal wear, the big necktie inspired the full butterfly (club bow) or semi butterfly bow tie both in traditional black, midnight blue and the new white pique. These bow ties usually had square ends, which were a neater appearance against the simple tuxedo. These were contrasted with the very skinny ribbon bow tie and thistle tie. There was also the velvet tie trend in Britain. The 60s couldn't make up their mind on just one look.

If you like crazy patterns, then ties of the 1970s are for you. The earthy tones and plant life, large paisley and animal prints made of wool and polyester materials gave the ties a new texture. Once again ties expanded to about 4.5 inches wide, but longer this time, as trousers were worn lower on the waist, and in some cases on the hips. The inspiration was taken from '40s American ties, but this time the patterns were rainbows, swirls, and clouds in pastel hues.

One popular new tie in Europe was the neckerchief. A square silk scarf was tied around the neck and held in place with either a square knot or a tie ring with ends pointing to the sides. The hippies wore their neck scarves loose without a pin so as not to be confused with an actual necktie.

The rise of the no-tie was the trend for the '70s and would have continued had the conservative '80s not brought the rebellious youth back to society and into business suits, and power suits, once again. Influences from previous eras was clear, and the cyclical fashions gave to different looks depending on individual tastes. In contrast to the businessmen wearing loud, and often reasonably wide Paisley ties, you would often see young men wear very narrow ties. Sometimes these were even made of leather. Especially, as a Mod revival became popular amongst youth culture. Pop stars would also wear narrow ties, and you only have to see The Jam, and Paul Weller, to see how much influence the look with narrow ties had on a new generation getting into style. Funnily enough. When the Jam first started Paul Weller hadn't fully transformed into the Mod icon he would become. There are some photos of him with a long early 1970s hairstyle, black shirt and a very wide tie with a Windsor knot. But, as he studied his craft and cottoned on to the whole sixties Mod thing, but, with a late 70s Punk edge, so he dressed not unlike Modern Jazz musicians of the 50s. Black suit, white shirt and narrow tie. Although, Paul's main influence was actually The Beatles, and their own take on style, and a sharp modern look.

As we move away from the 80s – ties became a bit more muted and more of a normal width. By the Noughties we see ties getting narrower again, and a reappearance of the knitted tie. Today, fashion is about individuality, so anything goes when it comes to ties. Vintage, and hipster styling has seen a re-emergence of ties of all widths, styles and fabrics. In fact, a couple of years ago I even saw and advert for a wooden tie! (Thankfully the gimmicky style didn't catch on.)

Today, in the workplace, ties are rarely worn, and the usual occasions to wear a necktie are those more formal events where it is usually expected. They are seen as a respectful nod to old conventions and are still De rigueur at such events. But there are still those who see a tie as a piece of clothing that not only elevates one's outfit, but actually says look at me, I am about style. Advertising, and fashion will still often show a person wearing a tie, it is still expected to be worn by male newsreaders for example, and the wearing of a tie is a tradition that is unlikely to completely disappear especially as they do have a use, for they can flatter a person's shape when worn properly, drawing the eye and giving the sharpness that you would expect from a sharp vibrant blade of silk.

A Link To The Past – A Brief History About Cufflinks

We sometimes forget the impressive history behind some elements of fashion and style. From the earliest evidence of woven fabrics, bone embroidery needles and shell jewellery, to the overhaul of manufacturing methods in the Industrial Age. Embellishments have evolved, and some styles have fared better than others, and have proven to remain for centuries. In fact, items manage to attain that hallowed position of tradition, and we have become so aware of their existence that we do indeed forget how or why they came about, or just adhere to the notion that their function is simply what it is for, or in this case what we are often told. The actual history isn't given real thought, it is just taken for granted. Accessories that have become traditional are typical of this. Their function often makes their history easily less important. For, after all it is the occasion that the wearer is wearing them for, that is truly relevant to the wearer at that particular time.

This article endeavours to look at the history of Cufflinks. The history is a fascinating one. One, with roots that go way back. In fact, as far back as the 13th century.

In the 13th Century, before the dawn of buttons, people would tie and secure their clothes with what they had to hand; a creative mix of string, pins, belts and ribbons – almost like the novelty cufflinks you can find today. As trends changed and people moved towards more fitted styles throughout the century, buttons emerged and were used as a more efficient, practical fastening that could still show social status based on the material and level of detail in the design.

In the 16th Century, as the Renaissance elite favoured fuller fashion, they embellished their garments with ruffled collars and frilly lace cuffs. Fashion had become more about pomp and circumstance than the practicality of the Middle Ages. This ornamental and opulent style influenced the following centuries, encouraging people to find a happy medium between the practicality of fitted and fastened clothing and the appeal of decorative elements.

By 17th Century, fashion was toned down in the post-Renaissance world, with men especially opting for less decoration and more simplicity. Cuffs were slenderer and more functional, though still capable of housing a status symbol for the best-dressed class. For nobility, cuffs were initially tied together with ribbon as a subtle nod to status, but it didn't take long for ribbons to give way to opulent jewelled buttons which quickly grew in popularity. Could this century be the birth of the classic cufflink?

By the Georgian era in the 18th Century, the sleeve buttons had become even more ornamental. Intricate and expensive, this was still a style choice for the elite, but it was starting to show a more playful, individual take on fashion with the addition of coloured gems and miniature hand-painted masterpieces.

The 19th Century Victorian fashions reflected the emerging middle classes, with grand aspirations on modest budgets. Luckily, the Industrial Revolution overhauled the production methods for clothes and accessories, making these pieces more widely available. The chains that were the usual link on cufflinks were replaced with rods and fasteners with easy-to-close clips. Many shirt makers were eager to sell a larger quantity of higher priced dress shirts caught on to the cuff link frenzy and expanded their lines of formal dress shirts to include cufflink-ready attire. Sales boomed and men flaunted their personalities in true Peacock style, as they sported their new look with cufflinks and matching stud sets. Imitation gems allowed for replicas of popular styles, while people sought alternatives to precious metals for settings.

By the mid-1800s, the classic French and double cuffs were a top choice, influenced by a romanticised ideal of historic French heroes. By the end of the century, both single piece buttons and cufflinks were in mass production.

The 20th Century was a busy century for the cufflink.

Enamelled cufflinks remained popular into the 20th century,

The Desired Article

but new fashionable movements turned functional accessories into masterpieces once more, with inspiration drawn from Art Deco and Art Nouveau designs, along with Faberge enamels.

By the 1970s though, dressing down and stylistic simplicity meant that shirt cuffs came with buttons already attached for ease. Cufflinks were limited to high-end labels and the haute couture world, where premier brands like Cartier and Tiffany's even incorporated their famed diamonds into favourite cufflink designs. By keeping cufflinks, a staple on the catwalk though, designers prevented the practice from fading out entirely.

The 1980s saw cufflinks make the news with a pair of Edward VIII's cufflinks selling for just over £115,000. He had been an advocate of Faberge cufflinks, but this sentimental pair were encrusted with Cartier diamonds, fashioned into an E and W – Edward and Wallis.

The 1990s saw the world embrace cufflinks once more. The French cuff was back, for men and women alike, and cufflinks topped off the look. They were an accessible statement piece for all ages and styles; from power-dressed businessmen to women experimenting with androgyny and tailored styles. This was also the resurgence of preppy fashion, with clean-cut shirts and chinos from brands like Hilfiger and Lauren proving popular. Cufflinks supplied an easy way to personalise the everyday preppy look.

The 21st Century is undoubtedly the age of anything goes! Styles are more varied than ever, with influences from every era playing into our fashion choices. When it comes to cufflinks, creative twists on timeless classics are keeping the tradition alive, while more unique designs provide customers with the new versions of wrist wear that we see available today. Men are swapping chunky watches for cool mechanical cufflinks and women are trading delicate, sometimes impractical, bracelets for edgier cufflinks set with precious stones. The majesty of cufflinks continues, and most likely in these post Pandemic times, when socialising is possible, the yearning for a smarter style will return, and cuff links will no doubt feature when considering outfits for particular occasions, or that touch of personal flair if required to wear formal outfits in the workplace.

Fabric cufflinks:

> An alternative type of cufflink is the cheaper silk knot, which is usually two conjoined Turk's head knots. The Paris shirt maker Charvet is credited with their introduction in 1904. French cuff shirts are often accompanied with a set of colour-coordinated silk knots instead of double-button cufflinks. They are now often not made from silk, but of a fabric over an elasticated core. Due to the popularity of this fashion, metal cufflinks shaped to look like a silk knot are also worn.

Motif's:

> The visible part of a cufflink is often monogrammed or decorated in some way, such as with a birthstone or something which reflect a hobby or association. There are numerous styles including novelty, traditional, or contemporary styles.

One particular style I like is that of the wrap around cufflink. It just ads a bit more interest and richness to the cufflink. For some this may seem too much of an affectation. But, to other likeminded people, such an added detail is appreciated. It shows a little bit more thought has gone into the outfit. It's foppish dandyism accentuating a personal individualism. They first appeared in the early 1940s and were extremely popular through to the 1970s...and have been rediscovered by today's cuff link wearers. These unique cufflinks feature a wrap-around device which wraps around the shirt cuff and elegantly joins the front and back of the cuff link. Usually, the device would be a matching metal mesh, or chain. I did see a gentleman wearing a pair that had a strip of leather wrapping around the cuff from the front to the back of the link once, which I found fascinating and different in terms of design.

That Touch Of Class — The Pocket Square

I feel it adds a touch of class and individuality, whilst helping to tie an outfit together.

Why do we wear these pocket squares and where does this classic men's accessory come from?

It was it seems, the Greeks. Yes, the same Greeks who have given us so much throughout the ages, such as Democracy, Geometry, Philosophy, and a rich history that fascinates us all so very much.

The Desired Article

Around 500 BC The Greek hierarchy meant that Greece's richer citizens decided to carry perfumed handkerchiefs on their person. This protected them from the not so pleasant smells, originating from the dirty streets and the poor beggars who unfortunately lived on them. A seemingly natural development for those who were fortunate to live in their grand spacious airy homes, and yes – the elite privileged, were rather snobbish, even back then.

However, there is no evidence that they invented the handkerchief, as an essential accessory, this really came much later.

Apparently, it was our main man King Richard II, the ruler of England who invented it a few years later. It is he who is said to use a little piece of cloth to wipe and clean his royal nose and as history always shows, it wasn't long before the upper classes in England followed suit. By the 17th century, the handkerchief was common amongst all the classes throughout western Europe and the solution to everyone's runny nose had well and truly been found. Something not to be sniffed at!

Originally, the handkerchief was kept in the trouser pocket. As presumably no one wants to see your dirty cloth, regardless of how proud you may be of it…

It wasn't in fact until the two piece suits came into fashion in the 19th century, that men started to place their clean pocket squares into their jacket outer dress pocket. In order to protect it from coins, lint and general dirt, that would also be found in their trouser pocket.

Over time, the different types of folds used to place the pocket square became more elaborate and fancier and the pocket square made the transition from a useful practical item, to an aesthetic feature.

Such was the case that many men started to carry two around

with them. One for show like a peacock, trying to catch the eye of the ladies and the second for more practical uses. Like offering it to a distressed lady, helping to comfort her when she is crying or wiping ones brow after a long day's work.

During the 1940's and 50's, the linen handkerchief fell out of favour and in its place, the disposable handkerchief made by Kleenex became the popular choice. As a result, the linen handkerchief was replaced and only used as a fashion accessory, in the form of a pocket square. Since then, a variety of fabrics have been used. Many of the more expensive and more elaborately patterned pocket squares are made of silk, and there was a period when a matching silk pocket square and silk tie was popular.

At events when a Tuxedo is worn, a simple white pocket square is often the requirement.

So that is the story of the humble pocket square from practical cleaner upper/ bad smell preventer, to a fashion accessory.

During the 21st century, pocket squares have enjoyed something of a renaissance and have become an essential accessory for fashionistas, celebrities, and anyone who really wishes to stand out from the crowd and add a touch of style and elegance to an otherwise ordinary suit. Mods in particular are renowned for their sharp dress codes, and the afore mentioned elaborate folds have often been a part of a Mod's armoury, when adding individual flair, and style to their outfits. Suedeheads, an evolved style conscious tribe, who came out of both The Mod, and Skinhead scene would also wear pocket squares in the chest pockets of their Crombie overcoats. A look that added flair to their sharp clean look.

A pop of colour protruding from ones breast pocket has become a touch of class, a badge of true style that can represent an individual's personality. The more flamboyant the square, the more a person is seen as a flamboyant individual. Modern dandyism an expression of that individuality.

Here is half a dozen of the many different folds that can enhance your style.

The first is a very simple one:

The TV Fold.

The TV Fold (also known as the Presidential fold) is so named because of its popularity amongst American TV game show hosts in the 1950s. It's a simple fold that shows a straight line of ¼" (0.6 cm) to ½" (1.3 cm) of pocket square above the breast pocket.

Also, a popular fold seen worn by the Rat Pack, Frank Sinatra, Dean Martin, Sammy Davis Jr etc. during this time.

Then we have:

The Puff Fold

Allegedly invented by Fred Astaire, the puff fold gets its name from the cloudy, "puff" shape created when finished in the breast pocket. Once you learn the fold, it's one of the quickest to execute and punches far above its weight in style points.

This sort of fold is ideal for silk handkerchiefs with eye-catching patterns and designs. It's quite flamboyant and playful, without looking too contrived.

Next there is:

The Simple Fold Over:

This fold is simply a slightly asymmetrical TV fold with the handkerchief's edges facing upwards. Easy to execute while simultaneously sartorially conservative and visually interesting, it works particularly well with white hanks that have a coloured hand rolled trim.

The fourth is:

The One Point Fold:

Another easy-to-fold number, one point looks like a triangle pointing upwards from your breast pocket. A bit more complex than a TV fold, it's a tad more conspicuous as well. Overall, it works particularly well with solid squares. This fold is followed by the Two Point Fold:

Needless to say, the two-point is very similar to the one-point fold above, but with two points showing up from the pocket. When the number of points increase so does the complexity of the fold, and it begins to look more contrived. That said though, a well-executed pocket square with 3, 4, or 5 points adds a level of detail that can be admired by pocket square fans. It shows a certain pride and sharpness that simply has to be admired.

The last in this list is known as the Plop.

Cary Grant was known for this. It's essentially a non-fold, a version of the puff that's been stuffed into the pocket as opposed to folded. This "fold" is very casual in nature and goes very well with casual looks like odd jackets and trousers, sports coats worn with button-down collar shirts, and so on. It is a particularly laid-back and easy-going style, which simply exudes the laid back nonchalance of Sprezzatura. Something that is to me the embodiment of cool.

Tootal Scarves – A History Of Elegance And Modernism

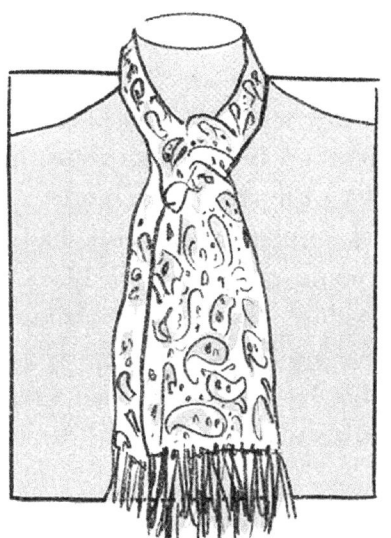

The British brand most associated with Mod scarves, and Cravats can trace its roots back to 1799 and Robert Gardner, a textile merchant and quite possibly the most stylish man who lived in Manchester at that time. With the arrival of steam power and canals Manchester – or "Cottonopolis" as it was nicknamed in the 19th Century – thrived as the centre of the textile industry. In

1842, Edward Tootal, "a merchant in silks and fancy dress materials" joined the rapidly expanding successful business.

Edward actually proved to be so successful, that in 1847, a mere five years later, the company was renamed Edward Tootal & Co. When he retired in 1856 the business passed to his nephew, Henry Tootal Broadhurst, and Henry Lee, who had originally been an apprentice to Robert Gardner.

When it comes to the history of Britain's textile industry, it is not complete without mentioning that in 1862 workers at Lancashire cotton Mills actually refused to handle raw cotton picked by US slaves, despite the impact it would have on their own welfare. The following year in 1863, President Abraham Lincoln would write an open letter to "the working men of Manchester" praising their "sublime Christian heroism which has not been surpassed in any age or in any other country".

By the end of the 19th century Tootal had three large textile mills at Newton Heath in Manchester, Black Lane in Radcliffe and Daubhill in Bolton. The thriving business, that used beautiful cloth and very principled people was joined by beautiful architecture when in 1892 Tootal opened a large new brick-clad warehouse and office block, in Oxford Street, Manchester. In 2017 it was announced that the Mayor of Greater Manchester – Andy Burnham – would move his offices to this magnificent Grade II listed building, now known as Churchgate House.

Going back to when World War One broke out, Edward Tootal Broadhurst, Tootal's company chairman, joined the committee organising the Manchester Pal battalions. Tootal Broadhurst Lee & Co offered to keep jobs open to any of their workers who volunteered.

In 1918 Sir Edward was knighted for his contribution to the war effort. By way of thanks for local people's efforts during the war Sir Edward donated 80 acres of land at Broadhurst Park, Moston to Manchester Corporation. The area now includes the home ground of FC United of Manchester, who play in the National League North.

Tootal continued to work hard and thrive. The company was on a worldwide mission to dress the dapper and the dandy, and by 1939 had opened offices in Belfast, Birmingham, Leeds, London and Glasgow as well as overseas in Argentina, Australia, Canada, France, and New Zealand. In 1952 a new Total factory also opened in Devonport, Tasmania and by 1973 Tootal Ltd was reported to be the 9th largest cotton firm in the world, 5th largest in the UK, with 25,000 employees worldwide. They had a wide range of products including, ties and manufacturing shirting fabrics. Their scarves, ties and Cravats are what they are however most known for.

Today they work from a slightly more modest facility in Derbyshire, still making their famous scarves and accessories from 100% silk, and still applying the standards and skills they had mastered over the last 200 years.

According to Hardy Amies in, The ABC Of Men's Fashion (1964)

A scarf is "Crossed over at the neck, and usually in silk, is worn on the Continent more than in this country. I suspect it goes back to a habit of trying to keep the shirt collar clean and not in touch with the overcoat collar. If worn for warmth it looks more elegant worn turned over, muffler fashion. Many English men favour this."

And indeed, with England having a much cooler climate than the "Continent" Silk scarves were more often than not worn in this turned over muffler style.

The patterns on these scarves and the colours on them became louder with the evolvement of style and fashion, and many of Tootals scarves have seen their popularity grow due to elaborate Paisley patterns, the use of polka dots and geometric patterns.

Mods and Dandy's were naturally drawn to this. The ever style conscious young men saw a silk scarf as not just an accessory, but in some cases as a statement piece on an outfit. It worked as a subtle signifier to other Mods, that they were themselves a Mod. Mod after all was about adopting Continental style, and American styles and making them their own.

Initially the silk scarf was worn with smarter more tailored outfits, in the manner that the upper-classes would wear an often white silk scarf, when going to a formal event. But as these finely dressed men became more casual, they would add a scarf to an outfit for both practical reasons and as a fashion statement. By the time we hit the latter end of the twentieth century and the early twenty – first century, we see people like Liam Gallagher of Britpop band Oasis adopting the scarf as an iconic piece of his wardrobe. So much so, that when he forms his own clothing label Pretty Green, the silk scarf is a constant piece within its collections. Tootal have collaborated with Mod related brands such as Fred Perry in the past and subsequently are more known as being the go to brand for the original quality, as they were the original and often seen as the best for making these simple accoutrements. Of course, Tootal were not the only brands. Duggie, and Sammy were two well-known brands that did their own versions of the Paisley, fringed scarf. Many of which were two sided with a woollen side for added warmth. These tend to be bulkier than the Tootal Scarves when folded over and for this reason, I have always preferred a more streamline flatter folded silk scarf. There are many great independent scarf makers out there who produce Tootal inspired scarves, and Tootal still produces fine quality silk scarves for the style conscious.

In these days of Covid 19, perhaps a nice Tootal can serve as a face covering when going to purchase something in a shop. Now, that is an idea... I need to buy a new scarf...

Don't Be Stingy – Tell Me About The Pork Pie Hat

I am a fan of hats, I probably have too many, after all I only have one head. But for me a good chapeau can make a person stand out in a crowd. It can elevate their style and can help a person display a confidence that is admirable. Now, I am talking about real style. Not just a functional thing to put on one's head to protect yourself from whatever a person feels their noggin needs protection from.

Today, although many people will don a hat of some sort, it isn't a requisite for everyday life, unless it's part of a working uniform. Hats go in and out of fashion all the time. The period of that feeling of not being dressed properly without one, has almost been consigned to history. In this article I am going to write about a few of the styles of hat that are still relatively popular and have been considered as emblems of cool. First, there is the Pork Pie, and then there is the Stingy Brim Fedora, and it's similar looking cousin the Trilby.

The Pork Pie hat came into fashion approximately around 1830 and was first seen on the heads of American and English women and remained en vogue throughout the period of the American Civil War. In the early 1900s, this style changed gear and was seen on fashionable men out and about in town in Britain. American men, often enamoured by British fashions, soon adopted the pork pie style in the 1920s thanks to silent film star Buster Keaton, who wore them in many of his films. The popularity of the pork pie then continued to grow, through the American Great Depression until the end of World War II (when it topped many a zoot suit). It still remains popular within African American jazz, blues and ska music culture today, where it has retained many of the 'cool cat' associations it achieved throughout the 1930s and 40s.

The name "Pork Pie is, logically as it suggests, is because the hat looked like a pork pie sat on a plate, which was something seen regularly during the 19th century in the windows of most bakery's in England, during that period in history.

Although, in the second half the twentieth century its popularity began to decline, and the Pork Pie became considered as part of a particular look – that of the aforementioned Zoot Suit, and it's adoption by the African American music scenes, such as Jazz and Blues. It's association with cool music styles meant that this particular style of hat has remained an emblem of cool styling.

The death of jazz saxophonist Lester Young (who, often wore a Pork Pie hat on stage) saw, Charles Mingus, the jazz musician, and composer, compose an elegy for him called "Goodbye Pork Pie Hat". But, this was not the end of the style.

Between 1951 and 1955 this hat was seen on television as a part of the wardrobe of many celebrities such as Art Carney and Joaquín Monserrat.

In Jamaica, during the 1960's it was popular as part of the "rude boy" street style, and subsequently, thanks to the links in Britain with Jamaican communities, we also see the Pork Pie hat brought back to Britain and gain in popularity once more in the country.

After the 1960s, Pork Pie hats would reappear in popular culture in various manners. Yogi Bear wore one in the popular cartoon. Gene Hackman wore a Pork Pie hat in the 1971 film The French Connection and in 1973 Robert de Niro in the movie "Mean Streets".

During the 80s many pop stars would incorporate the Pork Pie into their celebrity outfits, as some fashions from the past became popular, albeit in often exaggerated ways. You only need to look at Kid Creole and The Coconuts, with August Darnelle in his Zoot Suits and hats to see how inspiration from the past was used and sometimes reinvented. Throughout popular culture since, they can be seen in photo shoots, in magazines, in music videos etc. More recently we saw the main character from the TV drama Breaking Bad wear a black Pork Pie hat, and the style is one that seems to remain popular, albeit not as popular as the Fedora and Trilby.

No two hats are mistaken for one another so much as the Fedora and the Trilby. Nor have two hats ever stirred up so much controversy as these two hats. This confusion and controversy, however, are by and large because of a lack of understanding over what a fedora and a trilby are, what their shape is, and the best way to wear either of the hats.

The fedora is a hat that can be first found mentioned in the last years of the nineteenth century and is not just part of the same hat tradition as the slouch hat of the mid nineteenth century and the homburg of the late nineteenth and early twentieth century, but also their natural evolutionary descendent. Popular from its inception until the popularisation of hats in the '70s, the fedora remains a classic hat.

The great popularity of the fedora arises from the fact that it can be both a casual and a dress hat, and the materials from which it is made reflect that. Wool felt and fur felt are both popular, and most fedoras shown in film are wool or fur felt, but straw, especially Panama Straw and raffia are good for summer wear.

A high quality material and construction for the fedora is a must. The crown is usually four or four and a half inches, with a pronounced "pinch" in the front of the crown. A fedora has either a "teardrop" or a "centre dent" crown, and these ornamentations are pressed an inch or two into the crown of the hat. Although a short, or "stingy" brim has been popular from time to time, a classic fedora has a brim between two and two and a half inches. A wide, or "generous", brim of three or more inches has also become recently popular. The brim is always a "snap" brim, meaning that the front or the front and back of the fedora can be snapped up or down, for styling or to protect the wearer from the elements.

Available in practically any material popular for hats, the Trilby is a naturally more casual hat, and as a result tends to be made from more inexpensive materials such as cotton, straw, raffia, and wool felt. Unlike the fedora, which has a movable, or "snap" brim, the trilby is made so that the brim is permanently fixed down, and usually the brim is set at a much more severe angle than the fedora. The crown of the trilby is the most identifying feature, and is angled inward more from the brim to the crown than the fedora, and the crown itself is either much taller but usually much shorter than the fedora. Like the fedora, the trilby does have a "pinch" and either a "centre dent" or a "teardrop" crown, but unlike the fedora all of these features are much less pronounced, almost to the point of nonexistence in some cases.

The trilby is a hat first popularized by a hat worn in a certain stage adaptation of George du Maurier's novel Trilby, and the name stuck. It was not at once popularised, but rather was worn as a "rich man's" hat in the early part of the twentieth century, and then mostly only in Britain. The Trilby hat didn't resurface until the 70s, when it appeared on the popular scene as part of styles that harked back to perhaps as much as two decades before, but it disappeared again, along with the popular wear of men's fedora hats and hats in general. The popular use of the trilby again resurfaced in the very early twenty first century, and it was it was from the trilby's use then that the confusion between the men's trilby and the men's fedora began.

What mostly sets the two hats apart is how they are worn, and it is the confusion about how these two hats are worn. As can be seen from its history and evolution, the fedora is a much more formal hat, but like a brogue shoe in modern street wear, it may be dressed up or dress down gracefully. The trilby, meanwhile, evolved from sportswear and trends, and is strictly to be worn casually. Badly worn Trilby's are often misidentified as a fedora, and the mistaken identity has caused the classic fedora some unfortunate public relations pain. Both the graceful men's fedora and the cool trilby are great looks, but each in a distinctive class unto themselves. Like the Pork Pie, Fedoras and Trilby's have been seen throughout popular culture over the decades. Especially in association with music and film. You only need to look at the likes of Frank Sinatra, in what can be also termed these days as Mad Men Chic (Popular TV series based on the height of advertising in Maddison Avenue), Nat King Cole looking sharp, or fictional figures played by actors such as Humphry Bogart, and Robert Mitchum in Film Noir movies wearing Fedora's to appreciate the styles.

When Two Tone became popular in Britain, so the association with style was evident. Often monochrome, the wearing of a stingy brim fedora or a trilby was commonplace by the bands, and the audiences alike. Again, Two Tone acknowledged the Rude Boy look, the Trilby or stingy brim Fedora were most likely easier to find than a genuine Pork Pie hat in Britain at the time, or at least in the working class urban environments of the Midlands where Two Tone really evolved. Hats can be an extension of personality, or something to help shield and disguise. Classic looks are often returned to, because of their associations. When watching a series such as the afore mentioned Mad Men, and I see Don Draper perfectly attired from head to toe, I appreciate the sharp style, just as I like the style of classic adverts by Knox in The Ivy Look by Graham Marsh and JP Gaul. I love looking at pictures of Jazz and Blues musicians, whether it be on an album cover, in a book or on a screen. I identify hats as being part of every well-dressed man's wardrobe. Especially if the style complements the attire and it emphasises a sense of cool.

The Accessory That Fits The Bill – The Money Clip

There are some accessories that have a gravitas that elevates a persona a little. It's not an essential item, and as we begin to move towards a cashless society, so they are becoming rarer, and generally only used by the wealthy who like to display their wealth, and use cash to pay tips, and for other items where cash is the favoured currency.

The money clip is essentially an optional fashion accessory that is more often used by men. Its job is that it keeps paper money sorted and prevents it from being rumpled-looking in your trouser pocket. There is without doubt a degree of style and flair attached to the use of this kind of clip. After all, if you are of the idea that you have a certain position, or a certain status, going out for a night on the town, it would not do to pay club cover charges with badly folded and crumpled up dollar bills. It is far more impressive to pull out a wad of neatly folded cash and hand the doorman the right change in the blink of an eye.

The history of the money clip is directly tied to the history of non-coin currency. Invented during China's Han Dynasty in 118 BC, original lightweight bank notes were made of leather. China was also instrumental in developing banknotes during the Tang dynasty in the seventh century. Europeans did not take a liking to paper money until approximately the 13th century. The banknote stuck around and has become more popular than coins, which are more difficult to carry due to their weight. Modern paper money is made from Polymer.

The new polymer notes allow for enhanced security features, such as the see-through window and holograms. This makes them harder to counterfeit than paper notes.

They're stronger, too: a polymer fiver is expected to last two-and-a-half times longer than the old paper £5 note. Although, while our notes are stronger, they are not indestructible – so you should still take care of them.

The life expectancy of polymer notes also makes them more environmentally friendly. The Carbon Trust has certified that the carbon footprint of a polymer note is 16% lower than its paper predecessor.

Finally, polymer notes are cleaner since their smoother surfaces are resistant to dirt and moisture. Also because of their smother surface, keeping your notes together in either a wallet or by using a money clip is prudent should you want to use cash. As stated though, cash is often used less than bank or credit cards and there is a possibility cash will all but disappear eventually, as technology advances. Another use for some of the smaller decorative money clips, is that of the tie clip. So, it's good to know that some 20th century money clips had a dual purpose!

An early precursor to the money clip is the drafts organizer of ancient Mesopotamia. Although it would be correct to say that this clip is more closely related in function to a paper clip, it does factor into the money clip's history by virtue of the items it secured. Back in 323 BC, a clip would be used to hold notes detailing the storage of grain. The clips prevented loss of papers and helped with the easy distribution of the notes. A similar clip was used in Japan until about 300 AD for notes detailing rice storage.

When money clips were used in connection with European paper currency, these devices were initially used to clip bills to the owner's clothing. This was a protection against pickpockets who would make off with loose wads of cash. Materials used included leather and bone. American money clips came into fashion right around the 1900s. Reserved for the wealthy, these clips were made of precious metals like gold or silver.

Modern money clips are a fashion accessory for the man who values a debonair appearance and loves to display flawless social graces. Modern clips may be made of copper, gold, silver and also platinum. Some feature personalized engravings. Marketers of high-ticket items have caught on to this fashion trend and have begun to use money clips as a means of advertising a store's logo or brand name. The use of these clips is for the practically-minded user but often a bona fide dandy who keeps a close eye on his personal appearance, will accessorise with such an item.

It adds to that sense vintage style and the idea of being properly attired. So, even though the money clip sits in a pocket, when revealed it shows the attention to detail, a well-dressed person wants to reveal. So, like a watch, cuff links, tie clips etc. It is the accessory that fits the bill it is intended for.

The Khaki Experiment And The Chino Cinch

OK, the title of this article could be mistaken for the ludicrous title of a mid-twentieth century pocket book novel. You know the ones that you could pick up from a newspaper stand for about twenty five cents in the US back in the day, when working men would read a book for entertainment? It would have a lurid cover with some "Dame" on the front, and maybe a hero or villain. The books would be bought mainly by men who were part of an era prior to the shooting of J. F. Kennedy in 1963, men that wore a uniform of sorts. It was what has been described as "Ivy Style". People, like President Kennedy, and high profile celebrities had become a role models for this style. Taken from the elite universities, the Ivy Style schools, such as Harvard, Yale, Dartmouth and Princeton etc. You would see men of all ages wearing elements of this style that has now become the classic reference point for menswear sophistication and class during work, rest and play. One component of this was the Chino. A cotton trouser that can be worn in a variety of ways. They can equally dress down an outfit, as well as smarten it up. It's traditional colours, especially that of Khaki, (I will come to that shortly) made them a versatile everyday trouser suited to the male wardrobe. Here, I am going to look at where the term for the name of the trousers "Khaki's" came from, and how, the style of them has changed very little over the years, as this still popular garment gets reinvented for each new generation.

So, where does the term Khaki begin?

It actually begins in British Colonial times in India, and not surprisingly has its association rooted in the British military. It is said, that around 1845, the soldiers would deliberately stain their white uniforms, with mud. Considering how a brilliant white uniform would make a person stand out, and therefore become a target. It was a very wise thing to do. Using the mud, dust and coffee, and perhaps curry – uniforms were customised to be darker and less visible in the terrain that the soldiers were working in. The term "Khaki" actually means "dust" in Urdu. Another theory of the invention of the garment and will perhaps explain the often lighter weight of some chinos (remember practicality is usually the key to many styles) is that the commander of the British forces in the Punjab, Sir Harry Lumsdon, replaced his regulation uniform trousers, as he found them too heavy in the hot climate, for a pair of lighter weight cotton pyjama trousers, which he dyed with tea leaves. Creating the dusty colour that we know as Khaki today.

By 1848 the British military had adopted the practicality of "Khaki" or "dust" coloured uniforms and had made it the regulation colour for uniforms in hot climates as found in campaign's in India, South Africa, Sudan and Afghanistan. Initially the uniforms were manufactured in China. It was believed that by having them made in the Far East, and shipped to the Middle East, transportation costs would be reduced. However, maybe because of quality, or the logistics of the transportation it was decided that in 1850 such uniforms could be manufactured within the British Empire. After all, textile manufacturing at this time was something the British were well known for. Britain had just a decade earlier been going through the tail end of The Industrial Revolution, a period when Britain was a world leader. Especially in manufacturing.

The first reference to chinos came later in 1898, when American armed forces were stationed in the Philippines during the Spanish-American War and their uniforms were sourced from Chinese twill cotton, very much in the way the British had their first Khaki uniforms made in China. This term "Chino" was born from the local language, and Spanish name for "China."

With the American forces adopting Khaki, so, we see more development. When we come to 1941 during World War II, the Khaki trousers are made from a tough, hard wearing twill called Cramerton, which is created by weavers Galey & Lord. Officers in the US approved a more extended use of Khaki's so, that they could be worn at "downtimes" not just during essential duties. Their comfort and practicality making them a garment that most men were happy to wear no matter what the occasion, unless it was a formal event.

After World War II, returning GIs began wearing the plain-front trousers pretty much all the time, they had become so habitual to wear, and chinos were soon seen as a common sight on college campuses, where they began to define the East Coast, Ivy League aesthetic. Hollywood soon followed, and as in previous articles, the power of celebrity cannot be underestimated, film stars wearing Chino's looked cool, and men of every generation has always wanted to buy in to that, therefore leading a generation to define chinos as a symbol of effortlessly cool American style.

With the growing popularity of the usually flat fronted cotton trouser known as Chino's, so some American companies began to produce their own versions. One such is Levi's who began to produce them as early as 1906 under the Sunset label.

Chino's did go through a period where the fashion of the day changed silhouettes considerably during the eighties and nineties. As a consequence, you began to see looser Chino's with pleated fronts. Moving away from the more military aesthetic and towards a more European look. As a consequence, at the time Chino's became less popular, and were seen as a more old fashioned garment associated with the older generation. However, since the nineties they have very much made a steady comeback. In fact, during the last decade, they seem to be everywhere. This is not surprising really, as popular fashion has become a little less formal in more recent times. So, the practicality of Chino's has made them a popular garment again. Lighter in weight than denim, and very comfortable and now available in a wide array of colours, and more contemporary widths, to suit all tastes they have become something of a staple in many a man's wardrobe. However, it has to be said, there is those that always want to be a bit different, and not follow the crowd. Authenticity, or just a slightly different detail makes some individuals want something that is no longer readily available at a reasonable price. I have to hold up my hand and admit, I am one of those people. For me, it is a pair of Levi's cinch back chinos. I think that perhaps this little detail which has been seen on garments such as denim jeans over the decades has made them almost a holy grail to me. I mean. Sure – If I search hard on various vintage sites, and in old books and catalogues, I may find cinch back chinos. But they are usually reproductions. Not the elusive original Levi's that I see in old images and adverts. Having been influenced by Ivy style and brands that British Mods like for over half of my life. It is the Modernist love affair with Levi's that makes them appeal to me. However, there is a now a rare and once popular US brand that quite possibly did the Cinch back Khaki first, and that is the one I wish to draw your attention to now.

It seems that the American collegiate brand H. I. S. Are to be credited with putting a Cinch back on their trousers in the early 1950s. Not, Levi's as I originally presumed.

Jesse Siegel is credited with creating the Cinch back. Siegel was the first to take khakis, the by then, old-time favourite in work clothes, and put a buckle on the back, so as to aim it towards the youth market. An advertisement by H.I.S from 1958 makes an interesting claim. The advertisement is for a new line of back-flapped khakis called the post-Grads and plays one trend off against another. The copy reads "H.I.S introduced the Ivy-Alls six years ago and saw them become the biggest style idea in the history of men's slacks. We still turn them out by the thousands every week, but the future belongs to the post-Grads." The copy goes on to say, "the buckle-on-the-back has yielded to a pair of neat flaps." This advertisement places the introduction of the belted back Khaki trouser as early as 1952.

Siegel was quite a good baseball player and had a try-out with the New York Yankee's farm team. The Baseball gloves he wore at the time had a buckle back strap which you could tighten to fit your wrist and hold it snuggly in place. It is rumoured that this is where the idea came from. How true this is, is hard to say. But the story does have a plausibility about it.

There are many brands that do Chino's or Khaki's today, one such brand is GAP, who ran a fantastic advertising campaign many years ago with notably cool icons wearing Khaki's. One such image in the campaign is an image of one of my favourite authors, the King of the Beats, Jack Kerouac. The image is a powerful one that has always stuck in my consciousness, simply because, Kerouac's writing is associated with what is considered "cool". Coolness plays a big part in marketing, and even old images can still purvey that sense of the elusive feeling that so many want to be part of. The advertisements are telling you that you can be as cool as Jack, if you wear a pair of their Khaki's. Which is obvious nonsense, but still we are seduced and are prone to parting with our hard earned cash to look like a hero. Whether it be one from the screen, or a real life hero who has inspired you by putting his life at risk for your safety and doing service for his country.

Now, as I stated. It is the Levi's version of a Cinch back I have been interested in. Why? Probably because I still associate Levi's as being "Cool", and a brand whose heritage I still like, just like the GAP example, Levi's is a label associated with a history of coolness. Unfortunately, these days the prices of LVC Chino's are very high, and my chances of getting a pair in the condition I want, is fairly slim. And, let's face it. If it wasn't. It would really be – a Cinch...

The White T-shirt — A Canvas Of Expression And Style

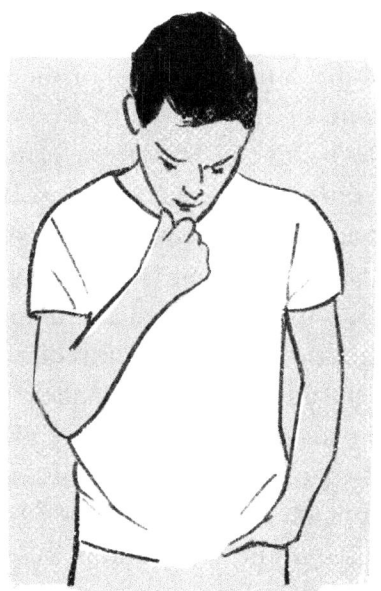

So, as the nation bathed in an Indian Summer, with beautiful sunshine during mid-September, so I take a look at a fashion staple. It doesn't belong to any particular style, although some style tribes may have appropriated it more than others. There is no doubt though, that at some point all of us will have worn one. Either simply to be cooler in hot weather, or as an extra layer beneath a shirt or sweater. I am of course writing about the simple white t-shirt.

How did the T-shirt become an essential feature in our wardrobes, and, perhaps as popular as say, a pair of jeans?

The most classic version, a white cotton jersey crewneck that became standard military issue in World War II, is, for those that do not know, descended from undergarments worn by Navy men during the early 1900s. Chanel famously adapted jersey, a fabric traditionally used for underwear, into fashionable womenswear in the twenties, but it would be decades before this hidden staple came out from under, and gradually morphed from a masculine to a unisex garment.

Once an item bought in bulk from Hanes or Fruit of the Loom, the undershirt grabbed the attention of the US Navy, and Hanes began producing white cotton T-shirts for the US Marine Corps in 1901.

By the 50s, it was still considered an undershirt, many, of the more conservative, and traditional adults didn't agree that it was proper to wear T-shirts in public. This made it the perfect symbol of youth rebellion, and, subsequently stars like James Dean and Marlon Brando began to sport the T-shirt on screen, most famously in the 1951 film A Streetcar Named Desire. Elvis Presley also brought the Tee to the stage, and in 1956, the rock 'n' roll icon created the first-ever band tee—printed, of course, on a white T-shirt.

Over time, the classic white tee moved past its humble origins.

The innovation of printing and embellishing T-shirts didn't really reach its peak until the 70s. Its ability to turn a simple garment and its wearer into a walking billboard was huge. It became a fast fashion staple in the 90s, Although, in the eighties it was quite prevalent in advertising. Who remembers Nick Kamen in the launderette with his Levi 501's wearing a black tee, obviously making a nod at 1950s/60s culture? Although, in the initial advert, the t-shirt isn't a white one – it shows that the t-shirt had a status for not only style, but as part of a young person's wardrobe. In fact, that advert alone not only added to the increased sales of Levi's, but to the sale of t-shirts, and a style of underwear that had not been fashionable for quite some time – the humble Boxer short.

Also, by the '80s, with the emergence of expressive mediums like tie-dye and the ever growing market for printed graphics, the tee had managed to garner and establish mainstream approval—from the Sex Pistols' iconic "God Save the Queen" print, to NYC's famous "I ♥ NY" souvenir T-shirt.

In the 90s the white t-shirt received another endorsement from high end fashion and the designer treatment from the likes of Karl Lagerfeld, who in 1991 layered Chanel's signature tweed cardigan jackets over white tees, and then, as t-shirt's had been so prevalent in youth cultures, you see in the early 90s, a continuation of many young people wearing t-shirts. This became even more noticeable with music artists, still wearing T-shirts, while performing on stage. Hip Hop T-shirt's for A.P.C. for example, became a sell-out success.

It is precisely this phenomenon that makes us appreciate, what this garment is: The basic tee, after all, is the simplest, easiest piece of clothing imaginable—its blank canvas quality functions like a screen on which we project our current cultural preoccupations. A T-shirt can signify working-class status; symbolise rebellion (James Dean in Rebel Without a Cause), athleticism (just ask any sports figure from dancers to boxers and everyone in between); emphasise sexiness (that cling!). And it's the most versatile piece imaginable too—the T-shirt can be worn anywhere, from the backwaters of New Orleans (Marlon Brando in A Streetcar Named Desire) to a night club in Manchester, (As I often did when I went to the Hacienda) A couple of years after I started frequenting the said club, one of the most iconic graphic tees was produced. With the advent of Acid House, so the Smiley T-shirt became hugely popular. The Smiley is also credited as being the first emoticon, of which there are so many today.

No wonder, then, that along with jeans, the classic white tee remains a key element of the quintessential casual-cool uniform to this day: Its very plainness, after all, leaves room for self-invention and a canvas for expression. Used for slogans, for advertising and as a style signifier. This item of clothing is one that will no doubt remain. In winter months, many people still wear it as an under garment. It can add to an outfit's subtlety – yet elevate it. Picture an Ivy style, Preppy look, where a crisp white tee is worn beneath an Oxford Cloth Button Down. The top button or two are undone, the flash of a white crewneck just peeping out. It's classic, it still looks smart, yet casual enough. The layers look right. Almost a timeless nod to the past of underwear. The cotton tee serves to wick perspiration away from the skin, and the outer garment. So, there should be minimal perspiration marks on the shirt. It's practical in the summer, when you don't want the heat. The sun bouncing off the white, or practical as an under garment in the winter. This versatility, and adaptation makes it possibly one of most important items in the wardrobe, it's just that for smartness sake, always think is it suitable for where you are going? If it is. You have your look down to a Tee.

From Wabash To Hickory, And A Bit Of Acid Jazz Style

There are many types of fabrics associated with work wear, especially originating in the 1800's when it was first mass produced. Everyone knows about denim, it's been time tested and worn throughout the ages – but what about the other types? Let's start off with one, that was, once upon a time really well known, but eventually faded away into obscurity. That fabric was a Native American fabric called Wabash, from West Virginia.

To a modern eye, a Wabash fabric might seem overly formal – almost like a pinstripe or chalk stripe you would see on a smart suit. – but in reality, this fabric was, alongside denim, worn almost exclusively as workwear. Forty years before the first pair of Levi's jeans were made, J.L. Stiefl & Sons of West Virginia were making their "Indigo Wabash Stripe."

Before Stiefl began making this fabric, the tribes of the Wabash Confederacy had made a name for themselves, making intricate, decorative patterns and selling these to white workmen, and establishing the connection between the beautiful, durable garments and the Wabash tribe.

Wabash fabrics were once made by block-printing the pattern with a "resist" and then dyeing the entire piece of fabric, but modern manufacturers use discharge printing, to bleach out the signature patterns in an already woven fabric.

J.L. Stiefl & Sons called their product "Indigo Wabash Stripe" and it was often characterized by an impressive assortment of dots, triangles and diamonds. A few examples of these can be found in "King of Vintage vol 3" by photographer Rin Tanaka, although this book is fairly rare and commands high prices these days.

Another, similar and more familiar is that of another workwear striped fabric, and that is that of Hickory.

Hickory stripes, like Wabash, were made for hard work. Most famously these were circulated by the popular denim brand Lee, this heavyweight seersucker fabric had many of the same virtues as denim. The fabric was tough, but breathable, and the pattern obscured stains. It was no small wonder that this tough-wearing material (as tough as hickory) was mobilized as the de facto uniform of America's railway workers.

There is an image of an American railroad worker imprinted on my mind from some old western film, that I can not remember the title of, the character would often wear a hickory engineer cap as well as hickory bib overalls, or what we would call dungarees at the same time. Legend has it that, in reality, these caps were originally made for engineers by their wives from cheap pillow ticking, but at some point, they were made from the stronger, but similarly striped hickory material.

Britain went through a period of embracing the American dream, thanks to post world war economy's and advancements in technology, with movies and television. Because other nations, and cultures became accessible, so, audience of movies saw the garments that Cowboys, railroad workers and Native Indians wore, as I have already stated. Hickory stripes were seen on screen, and in comics etc., and naturally garments were beginning to be imported more. We all know how denim has evolved into the staple of many a person's wardrobe. The Hickory stripe, and Wabash garments were seen in Britain less often. As we know, stripes or patterns can often go in and out of vogue with the consuming public. But there are always times when styles may seem to be become popular, or at least stand out.

I have fond memories of a Hickory stripe shirt that I bought from The Duffer Of St George back in the latter half of the 80s. Although I was brought up in Manchester, thanks to reading Face magazine, and I. D. magazine, I became interested in Acid Jazz, and a Funkier Soulful sound from London, rather than just listening to what a lot of my peers up north were listening to. It was thanks to articles in such magazines I became aware of DJ, Barrie K Sharpe. The shirt I mention, was just one of several items I had over the years from The Duffer Of St George label, (I especially liked their Yardie Cardies, and other types of knitwear they did, and their jackets during the early nineties. The brand had been at the forefront of that Acid Jazz era, sadly the brand got incorporated into the high street chain of Debenhams in 2007/8, where it consequently lost its funky club style edge, and morphed into more mainstream attire.) The said Hickory stripe shirt was most likely a design approved, or designed by Barrie Sharpe himself, who, along with Eddie Prendergast, Marco Cairns, and Clifford Bowen were the brains behind the London club scene inspired clothing label. Sharpe is truly a British innovator, a DJ, writer, and a man who gets what is going on, and is always moving forward on a path of his own choosing. He knows what he likes and will produce things that echo elements of vintage design, with a distinctive contemporary edge. Sharpe is currently the main man behind the brand, Sharpeye, London. A brand that has always made and used the cool, urban utilitarian workwear style, that has been popular to some, in the last decade, and is simply the style, he himself likes. It was as if he had a Masterplan...

The whole club wear thing went hand in hand with the music. When you see the vintage style inspired outfits that Acid Jazz groups like Galliano wore, you see the inspiration for style. The Duffer shirt I had, had a longish collar, western jacket style pockets, and was made to be worn untucked. With its hickory blue and white railroad stripe I thought it was cool, it made me feel hip. If I hadn't got rid of it due to the extra weight I have gained as I have got older. I would no doubt still wear it today.

In recent years, Work wear style, and vintage looks have boomed. But true stylists put a contemporary twist on it. That's why those that were into Acid Jazz in the eighties and nineties, made their fifties and sixties influences into thoroughly modern interpretations, it was a new sort of Mod revival, that was a melting pot of culture and style. It was how it should be. Wabash and Hickory stripes are part of style history and will always reappear alongside a style of music and culture for those that dig deep for inspiration, and endeavour to move it forward.

Chambray – The Versatile Comfort Of The Blue Collar, And Work Wear Style

Chambray is a fabulous fabric that offers the unique texture and appearance of denim, but without the density and weight. Denim shirts have been popular over the decades and can produce some very interesting fades but wearing denim shirts can mean sweating uncontrollably during the summer months – they are in my opinion, more suited to cooler climates, and autumn/winter. Chambray is a very good summer alternative.

Chambray, perhaps unsurprisingly, has a storied and centuries-old history. Have you ever wondered where the term "blue collar" came from?

Chambray's history begins as far back as the mid-1500s, as it originally found roots in the cambric fabric. Cambric is a lightweight plain weave fabric, that at the time, was made of linen. The cloth was originally made in Cambrai, a formerly-Flemish region in northern France. It was a high-quality cloth, and was often used for shirting, handkerchiefs, and for intricate pieces like lace and needlework. The term cambric is synonymous with "batiste," a term that also originated around the same time period.

Chambray stemmed from this plain weave linen like fabric, and the English spelling of the term first became widely known in the early 1800's. It was formally endorsed in places like the 1831 US Farmer's Bulletin:

"For outdoor work in mild weather, choose a material such as chambray, which is durable, firm enough to prevent sunburn, yet lightweight enough admit air and be fairly cool."

The fabric made its way into widespread American use in 1901, when the U.S. Navy first authorized the use of denim and chambray. From then on through World War II, it was commonplace to see sailors wearing chambray shirts and denim trousers. Workers all over the U.S. quickly adopted the shirting fabric, giving birth to the widespread term "blue collar."

If you've ever taken a close look at chambray fabric, then you will know that it has a signature pattern that gives it an almost grey or blue like coloured appearance. This comes from a coloured warp (usually blue) and a white weft in a 1×1 plain weave. The white threads running over the coloured threads give the fabric a certain depth, all the while maintaining a lighter weight.

Of course, chambray can be woven in different densities,

much like denim, and can come in other colours. Finely made lightweight chambray dress shirts are now, it seems, more commonplace than they ever were.

However, heavier chambray work shirts will always be a hit with people who like a little more heft to their clothing.

There are tangible benefits, too. Chambray is typically very soft and smooth to the touch due to a finishing process where the cloth is heavily pressed, which also gives it a subtle sheen.

Chambray is so popular these days that even the average shopper wouldn't balk at the thought of buying a shirt made from this fabric…even if they mistakenly call it "denim."

People that are more style conscious are aware of Chambray and will no doubt have items in their wardrobes. I myself have a wonderful Charles Caine tab collar shirt made of the fabric, and a Chambray Baracuta G9 Harrington jacket. But it doesn't just end at shirts and jackets. You can buy trousers, shorts etc. – and even ties!

Traditionally, a chambray shirt was only to be worn at the weekend with chinos or in the workshop, due to its inherently casual nature. Steve McQueen, Paul Newman and Robert Redford have all worn it onscreen, and notably Dustin Hoffman wears a Chambray button down in The Graduate. Yet another example of a fabric/style working its way into the consciousness of the public and giving style nods to the observant.

In fact, it's nature as workwear has to be realised. It was comfortable, lightweight and practical, hence the US Navy adopting it as part of their uniforms. These days it is acceptable to mix and match chambray with more tailored looks. It can be seen to make outfits look more comfortable and a little less formal yet offer a style that is almost subversive.

Fashionably workwear style has seen a boom in recent years,

as a mix of vintage styles and the enduring relationship with denim and chambray has meant that there are many "looks" out there. Music often plays a part in style It's not surprising when you see Kevin Rowland, and other members of the band Dexy's wearing such styles. Or Hip Hop artists wearing Chambray. Chain gangs from the 1900s onwards would wear outfits made of Chambray and denim, as would cotton pickers, working in the fields. So, with Blues music, and early rock and roll and other styles of music, you see photos of artists wearing such outfits that influence many people with their individual styles. Although fashions come and go – it seems that there will always be a use for Chambray. It's here to stay, because its practical, and you can make it as modern or retro as you like.

The Classic Enduring Style Of The Breton Top

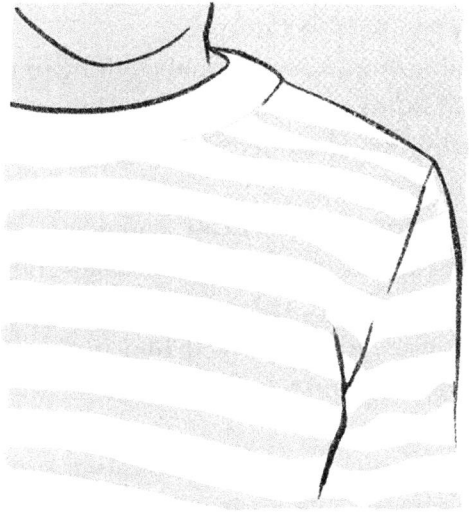

Sea-faring history has always influenced fashion – and no object more so than the Breton Top. But where did the history of the famous stripes begin?

Known today as a marker of chic and a stalwart of any Jean-Paul Gaultier collection, the striped Breton top was originally a knitted fishing shirt, designed to be worn for extra warmth.

The lightness of the top and the distinct stripes also meant that, were anyone to fall overboard, they would be easy to spot in the water.

Stripes were a popular design choice in the navy during the 18th Century, because of this factor, in fact the striped undershirt became part of the official French naval uniform in 1858. This is also partly where the name 'Breton' comes from – many of the sailors in the French Navy were from Brittany. However, the shirt in its uniform incarnation was known as the 'tricot rayé', meaning striped knit.

By the end of the century, knitted stripes were also a popular choice for swimwear across Europe.

The transition from occupational clothing to high fashion is often credited to designer Coco Chanel. Her early designs were based on the clothing of sailors, and she was well known for her love of the Breton.

However, it was an American couple, Gerald and Sara Murphy, who changed the game and successfully brought the striped top to the masses. They were friends of American composer Cole Porter, and they visited him in the French Riviera during1922, and liked it so much that they set up home there the following year.

It was whilst living there that Gerald took a trip to Marseille for some boat supplies and returned with the tricot rayé for his guests – who happened to include artists, authors and trendsetters such as Dorothy Parker, Ernest Hemingway and F. Scott and Zelda Fitzgerald.

It was from here, the popularity of the striped shirt as a fashion piece was soon seen to spread like wildfire.

But, getting back to Coco Chanel, the unintended, simple chicness of the Breton shirt was certainly not lost on this holidaymaker to the Brittany coast. On seeing fishermen wearing cheerful, striped shirts, Coco was hit with sudden inspiration. What she saw there by the sea inspired her 1917 couture collection – and Breton stripes featured heavily.

While Chanel may not have been the first designer to use Breton stripes in her designs, she was certainly the most well-known, and her androgynous styles based on modified menswear patterns are still worn today by the stylish, the comfortable, and the French.

Since the emergence of Breton stripes in high fashion, stylish celebrities have taken the look to new heights. From Picasso and Jean Cocteau to James Dean and Brigitte Bardot, the list of famous faces seen wearing this humble fisherman's jersey continues to grow to this day.

Style tribes such as Beatniks, and Mods have often been seen to wear the Breton stripe tops. Every summer season there is always a nautical element in many a designers collection. Breton stripes have become a casual staple in many a stylish person's wardrobe.

One of my personal favourites is a Breton shirt by Armour Lux, and as the brand sates,

> "The Breton shirt has become a signifier for a nonchalant, cool and effortless lifestyle – values that are reflected in the ethos of Armor Lux."

It is this nonchalant cool that makes the top timeless, and so appealing.

In more recent times there are many brands that have returned to this iconic look, and it is often seen both with high Street brands, and the more high end brands.

Another thing that makes a Breton stripe top stand out is the inclusion of a boat neck. It is said the wide, plain neck was said to ease quick removal if a sailor were to fall overboard. The style was adopted by the Russians and other navies in the following years. When Russian sailors adopted them, So, the Russian Navy adopted the style. Eventually, the Russian forces used them as undershirts for each part of the naval forces. They differentiated between Navy and Naval infantry for example by having different coloured stripes The Navy for The Navy, Black stripes for the infantry. Essentially tops are the same as the French versions, or at least very similar. The Russian version is called a Telnyashka. The aforementioned boat neck also makes Breton tops look cooler, and easily differentiates it from a normal knitted top or a simple T-shirt.

Capirari, did their own version of this wonderful casual style the other summer, and its classic look was quickly snapped up by style conscious aficionados, such as Paul Weller. It's structure putting a modern twist on the look that many people have enjoyed for many years.

I doubt the Breton top will ever go out of favour. I know that for me, it is a look that is clean and sharp. Teaming it with the right garments, always works.

Bermuda Shorts – A Legacy That Has Not Been Lost

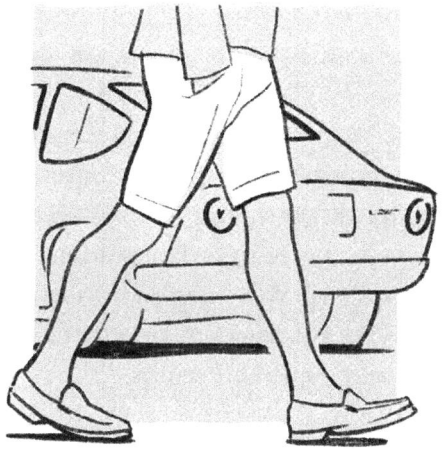

As we have recently been through a heatwave, I felt it was only right that I address a style of garment, that comes out every time the temperature increases, and it becomes practical to wear them. That garment is of course Shorts. Now, for this article I decided to focus more specifically on Bermuda shorts. Generally, the "Bermuda" (Not lost in the 'Triangle') is often dropped these days, and in the high street they are more often than not just called shorts. But why were they known as Bermuda shorts?

What is the significance, and why are they much more commonplace than you realise?

Bermuda is the only place in the world where they were the national dress for men. This changed however in 2007, when Bermuda decided to discard some of its British Colonial heritage.

Millions of people who have not yet visited Bermuda may think they know of Bermuda Shorts. But only the dress Bermuda shorts – what male Bermudians and professional business newcomers from all walks of life used to wear for business attire and cocktail parties in the evenings – These are the real Bermuda shorts, worn approximately three inches above the knee. They were often worn as a uniform, as day attire, and sometimes as informal evening wear, or walking wear.

Shorts owe the majority of their contemporary origins to the military. Quite possibly the earliest example of modern-day shorts, is roughly the 1880s when they are seen as part of the uniform of the heavily respected Gurkha soldiers of the Nepalese army — much like our Khaki (Chino) shorts of today, but these have four generous pockets and a distinctive cummerbund waistband with buckles and adjustable straps.

During World War I, Britain set up its North American Headquarters in Bermuda. It is said there was a single tea shop run by Nathaniel Coxon on the island, and because of the British soldiers, business thrived. The summer heat and the steaming pots of tea made the temperature inside the little tea shop more often than not unbearable. The owner, not wanting to spend money on new uniforms for his staff, took all the khaki trousers they wore, and cut them just above the knee. Rear Admiral Mason Berridge, who, so happened to like having his tea in this little shop, adopted the style for his fellow officers and soon christened them "Bermuda Shorts".

The Desired Article

The British Navy founded the yacht clubs in the port towns of Hamilton & St. George in Bermuda. And it wasn't long before officers of the British Army serving elsewhere began adopting the smart looking, summer version of the khaki military uniform. Before long, the men in London, who made such uniform decisions on behalf of the military, stated that standard dress was to be khaki shorts amongst all British soldiers serving elsewhere in the sub-tropics of The Old British Empire.

The local people of Bermuda soon began to notice the smartly dressed British officers milling around these yacht clubs, and it was not long before tailors began to copy and modify the style and make it appropriate for civilian use. This of course helped to establish the style, and by the 1920s it had become the standard business attire of the local men.

At this time, Bermuda was also a very popular steamship destination and tourists arriving for winter holidays soon helped to spread the style back to the United States and elsewhere around the world.

It has to be said, no country has influenced the school uniforms worn by children around the world more than England.

Originally, uniforms were first adopted by charity institutions to identify the children receiving charity. Only later, did exclusive private schools adopt the uniforms, with the goal of discipline and uniformity, but paradoxically, the uniforms served to famously identify the status of students from prestigious schools. With few exceptions, it was grey flannel shorts, based on the short trouser uniform worn by the British Military in Tropical settings.

The style was also adopted by the Boy Scouts, whose founder, Lord Baden Powell, himself a major General for the British Army. As these school children grew up and began to become adults in the world, gradually shorts became more acceptable in society, first, with outdoor activities like hiking and golf and then they made the very public jump to tennis. In 1932, when Britain's top ranked tennis player, Bunny Austin appeared in the U.S. National Championships in Forrest Hills, Long Island, he wore flannel shorts instead of the standard white trousers. This was much cooler for him, and the ability to move was easier and more comfortable. It was clear the style helped him. It wasn't long before other Tennis players also began to wear shorts.

After World War II, Western civil society began to shrug off the conformity that had been required. Society began to reorganise itself more, and by the 1950s, in suburban America, Bermuda shorts were seen as essential wear during the summer, and in the hotter areas of the country. Of course, this was also the period when Ivy style was at its height, and many Ivy League students adopted smart shorts when on campus. It seemed that Madras shorts were particularly popular.

These days there are several variations on shorts. Coming in various lengths, rather than the regulation three inches above the knee. Their practicality has insured a legacy of style. Thankfully we can say it was never lost in the Bermuda Triangle...

Throwing In The Towel With Style – From 007 To French Terry

For some reason, whenever towelling's mentioned, the first thing I think of is Sean Connery's baby-blue belted terry playsuit in Goldfinger (don't ask me why – some of you will already know I am a 007 fan). While I'd never endorse his romper – playsuit, I do wholeheartedly recommend the David Gandy for Autograph polo shirt, that I own, and bought a year or two ago.

It buys into that image at a price that was reasonable, and it is also well designed.

Part of Gandy's range of beachwear, it's made from premium, super-soft absorbent cotton and comes in Dark Navy, a Blue, that is as deep as the Med or a pale tone that is as white as the sand in the Caribbean. When I don this shirt, I feel at once transported to the glamorous Riviera's of the Sixties (Italian or French, you pick) – just add sunglasses, some swim shorts and a martini to nail that enviable movie-star cool.

Towelling or, I should say, Terrycloth, is the fabric we encounter at least once a day, when we step out of the shower and towel ourselves dry.

Terrycloth is best known for water absorption, making it the ideal choice for towels, robes, and iconic pre-pool playsuits. However, it's become altogether uncommon to see it used for much beyond the pool and beach sphere and has hardly ever been in men's clothing. Here, I will share a bit more about this less-than-iconic fabric and its slightly more modern and wearable cousin, which sounds like a character from a questionable bar or nightclub – French Terry.

Terrycloth and all its variants were born of a pre-industrialised French innovation by which the fabric was woven on a loom with not one, but two warp threads. One warp thread was left intentionally loose which, when pulled through the dense weft, formed loops on either side of the fabric, creating a piling effect. The first batches of terrycloth were made from silk, but eventually, the standard terrycloth would become the super-soft 100% cotton edition that we know and love today.

Starting in the 1850s, Samuel Holt's terrycloth knitting machines began churning out terrycloth at an industrial scale. The name terrycloth, it is believed, comes from the French verb "tirer," which means "to pull," and it certainly makes sense, given how the fabric is made. Its softness and absorption factor made it a clear choice for use in towels, especially considering before terrycloth's invention, people just used woven sheets of cotton or linen to dry off, which I should imagine was not anywhere near as comfy.

Although many will not be aware of the term French Terry, many of you will be very familiar with it – in the form of Sweatshirts, and sports and leisure wear. French Terry is basically a lighter and more pragmatic style of Terry towelling, where one side of the fabric is smooth and only one side has the characteristic pilling, we know and love. Though we've seen these used in modern sweatshirts regularly—with the smooth side facing out and the pile facing in for warmth – did you know French Terry was originally worn the opposite way?

As it was first worn on the French Riviera, French Terry was traditionally worn with the fuzzy, piled side facing outward and the smooth part inside. Though this partially defeats the towel-like purpose of normal terrycloth, these shirts merely emulated the style and were honestly worn by moneyed folk who weren't actually swimming all that much. French Terry is much more elastic than standard terrycloth and is nowhere near as heavy.

French Terry doesn't just make for good beachwear, it's also seen its fair share of sporty clothing, as already stated. That piled side turned inward is perfect for soaking up the sweat of a good workout, although nowadays, when many of us don't exercise, we will wear them purely for comfort. It is mostly just to add a little warmth to your favourite sweatshirt. French Terry is also more frequently blended with other fibres than its double-sided older cousin. It's not at all uncommon to add lycra, spandex, and sometimes even rayon to the mix

With the exception of certain brands like Drake's, most designers have shied away from bringing back terrycloth garments in any major way. When they do, they always have that 1930s French Riviera feel. Which I so happen to really like.

About few years ago, Orlebar Brown did bring out a very expensive Bond inspired range of clothes – including the 60s styling of Connery's Goldfinger playsuit, and other vintage polo shirts, and outfits. Making items that had only been seen on screen, more accessible to fans who could afford, what were in my mind very overpriced items, that were merely cashing in on the ever popular 007 phenomenon.

French Terry, it seems, is more prolific than ever. Though it is now worn in a markedly different and less beachy context, the fabric has found its footing in the world of pseudo-athletic comfy clothes, like the sweat suit, seen and worn by Rocky Balboa. You might go to the gym fully decked out these days in a heather grey French Terry track suit, also in this day and age, it has become commonplace to see, teenagers, and twenty somethings embrace a more leisure look style, so, its history remains evocative enough that many people have continued to wear it, even, if it's just for leisure rather than sport – much to the chagrin of many, as relaxed styles seem to have overtaken that true sense of style, that is evident from previous generations clothing.

As far as fashion and style goes though, the "Jocks" from US campuses, during the 50s and 60s, way before Sylvester Stallone appeared as the Boxing hero Rocky in January 1977, would mix athletic wear with their other Preppy and Ivy styles. So, it is, it seems that this evolution isn't really that surprising.

You only have to look at some images of students in Teryoshi Hayashida's book Take Ivy, and you see campus sweatshirts. Although the make up of these sweatshirts is different from that of French Terry and is more akin to what was created by the brand Russell Athletic, and later by another brand – Champion, they show the utilitarian and practical use of such garments. They are comfortable, keep you warm, and absorb perspiration.

But, I digress, perhaps really, the first use of terrycloth is still the most important and most common. That is of course, that of the humble everyday towel. Let's all give thanks for this innovation in softness and water-absorbing technology that so readily keeps us comfortable out of the shower and on the beach. The double-sided piled fabric might have never dominated menswear beyond the beachfront, but we do use the stuff every single day, and every summer some brand or other may produce a garment that has this quirk for those that want something a little different. I hope you found this an absorbing article. I'm off outside now to enjoy the sun, and drink a Dry Vodka Martini, whilst trying to outsmart a diabolical nemesis – and all the while, keeping myself as dry as the drink in my hand, thanks to, ahem- French Terry. Cheers.

A Tailored History Of Madras — Check It Out

No one will ever spill Ovaltine on those pajamas.

In fact they're the first pajamas I've ever seen that belong in the world of living breathing normal human beings. It's a funny thing. Most pajamas sanctify a man.

They really do. You take a nice normal guy and put him in dumb old pajamas and...thud...all of a sudden he looks scrubbed up and pure, and helpless, like a little boy waiting for mama to tuck him into bed.

That's no way to run a marriage. Good old Van Heusen. They understand.

This is how pajamas should look. Madras. Pow. All muscle and fit and glint in the eye.

There is no boy scout in this house. And I'll bet a nickel Van Heusen knows it.

VAN HEUSEN®
417 younger by design

The Desired Article

Many of those who are into the Mod scene appreciate what is termed as Madras. From shirts to jackets, to shorts and trousers, any astute Mod, Modernist, Ivy League fan, or stylish geezer should own something that is a summer staple among the stylish. Here is a short history of how Madras became popular in the Western world.

Madras is a breathable, beautiful fabric, and, its history, however, is fraught with imperialism, slave-trading, and even the naming of a certain famous American university. Madras, despite its enthusiastic reception by western colonial powers, remains a uniquely Indian invention, one that has adapted and morphed with changing tastes, but remains a testament to the indigenous ingenuity and artisanship of the region.

Most of you will be aware of the East India Company. The East India Company was the villainous organization we see in Pirates of the Caribbean.

It really was an actual British organization that was committed to plundering the natural wealth of England's richest colony: India. This real-life version of the organisation received its Royal Charter during 1600, and on its third round of expansion, set up shop in a colony called Armagon.

The Trading Company was doing much of its business in spices and textiles and the fabrics they discovered in Armagon turned out to be of an unacceptably low quality for export. The company was in a bind and needed to establish a new trading post with a thriving textile industry. In 1637, Francis Day, an administrator of Fort St. George and the city of Madras obtained a grant for the pre-existing village of Madraspatnam, leaving it under British control for at least two years. The port itself wasn't exactly ideal, as many British naval officers pointed out, but the high-quality, cheap cotton in the area was certainly the inspiration for such a calculated move. The trading post of Madras and its accompanying military installation: Fort St. George were established in 1639. The English managed to lure weavers and merchants from across the region with promises, such as exemptions from tax duties. By doing this, they, obtained some of the best hand-woven fabric available on the market at the time.

The British made a huge fortune in Madras. Firstly, by shipping the cheap, strong cotton, and then by selling an un-dyed muslin version, before finally recognising the real talent had been under their noses. The people of Madraspatnam had long been famous for the loosely woven and meticulously yarn-dyed fabrics.

The fabric that came to be known as Madras is, and was, woven by hand, first embroidered with elaborate patterns and later in more refined prints, in which red and blue were some of the most popular colours. Rice gruel was used as an adhesive and boiling spring water was used to set the dyes, the water of each region leaving a slightly different hue.

Records have shown that even before European presence in the region, the brightly-coloured fabrics were traded as far as Northern Africa and the Middle East during the 1400s. The sixteenth century saw this fabric refined to include more intricate dyeing processes and more complex patterns, but the Madras fabric was largely considered a working person's material and was seen as nothing particularly special.

By 1822, fabrics from Madras were mostly in various tartans, which had become popular after King George IV paid a visit to Scotland and found himself drawn to the pattern. The signature vibrant plaid of the Madras either comes from the presence of Scottish troops in the area, or simple Indian agency. It's just as likely that Indian weavers had created a plaid pattern entirely on their own – without any European interference, but as the plaid Madras fabric became a sensation back in Europe, the British did their best, unsurprisingly, to take the credit.

Yale:

The Collegiate School in New Haven, Connecticut was in dire straits when they reached out to the openly corrupt governor of Madras, India in 1718. The college wanted to erect a new building and turned to perhaps the worst-reputed man in the entire British Empire for help, Elihu Yale.

At the time of the college's request, Yale had a notorious reputation for enforcing a law that decreed that at least ten slaves must be placed on every boat to Europe. So egregious were his misdeeds that the British Government had to step in to try to control his predilection for illegally abducting local children and selling them as slaves.

Yale made a substantial donation to the ailing college. He sent money, books, paintings, and even yardage of the now-famous Madras fabric. The Collegiate School changed its name to honour the (frankly dishonourable) Elihu Yale and America had its first taste of the beautiful fabric that helped him earn his fortune.

Madras made a huge splash in the states, even after Elihu Yale's first gift had been entirely used up. A Sears catalogue from 1897 is one of the first tangible pieces of historical evidence about the fabric's reception in America. People evidently took to the stuff because by 1919, the New York Times was reporting a shortage in the U.S.

The easy-wearing, colourful fabric remained an affectation of America's rarefied leisure class. Many young men throughout the 1930s and 40s discovered Madras vacation wear while on trips to the English-controlled Bahamas. The simple, hand-woven, vegetable dyed fabric from modern-day Chennai, India slaked its wearer's desire to look and feel like colonial aristocracy.

Madras' big moment came with a 1958 fiasco when a fabric exporter did not explain to Brooks Brothers that the 10,000 yards of Madras they'd bought were going to fade. When consumers all over the country began angrily writing to Brooks Brothers complaining that their new jackets and trousers were fading and bleeding, the company summoned the exporter, Mr. Nair, to the United States to punish him.

But Nair deftly redirected their anger with an interview with Seventeen Magazine, in which he lauded the fading quality of this miracle fabric from India. Add some coverage by Esquire and Brooks Brothers had a huge phenomenon on their hands. Advertisers started praising the "marvellously muted" and "dustily well-bred" qualities of the Madras trousers and jackets. Before beat-up jeans were considered acceptable, a well-faded "Guaranteed to Bleed" Madras shirt conveyed a certain nonchalance that Ivy Leaguers loved. The reactive, unstable organic dyes that were nearly Madras' downfall were eagerly accepted and Madras proved to become an enduring American classic.

You can still find the bright patterned checks popping up at J. Crew and Brooks Brothers locations across America every spring.

But, it's not just the post war Mad Men on vacation style that we are talking about here. It's the way it was adopted in the UK especially by the Mods. Who lapped up the bright and interesting garments. Every now and then Madras, would pop up in a Hollywood movie, or on mid twentieth century television, whether it be as a shirt or jacket or shorts. By the sixties, the British Mods, often taking sartorial cues from both America, and Continental Europe, were drawn to the brightly coloured plaid fabric. Some bands in the sixties would even done a Madras blazer.

The Small Faces are a fine example of such a band., and photographs of the band wearing such blazers, still influence some of the choices a Mod may make when in search of a unique garment.

Of course – if it wasn't for the popular shops in London at the time, shops such as Cecil Gee, and of course those owned by John Stephen 'the King of Carnaby Street', beginning to stock, either actual, or copies of, American shirts, and blazers etc. And the look becoming more readably available. Then perhaps there wouldn't have been such a popularity with Madras.

John Stephen's, store His Clothes, and subsequent stores such as Domino Male, Mod Male, and Male W1, used a fast turnover of style that made the businesses popular with those who wanted to reinvent themselves on a weekly basis. When we see the Beat boom in the sixties, and then what was known as Swinging London, bands such as The Who, The Kinks, the Rolling Stones and of course The Small Faces would flock to the fashionable epicentre of London style and purchase their clothes. Famously The Small Faces manager Don Arden, who was not the most forthcoming with the money the band was earning, had his offices on Carnaby Street, directly above John Stephen's clothes shop and with an arrangement he had with all the menswear stores in Carnaby Street was basically able to offer The Small Faces shopping accounts as part of their contract, that and twenty pounds a week and a 'percentage' of their record sales. So maybe the most "Mod" band in the United Kingdom is particularly responsible for the popularity of Madras shirts and jackets on the scene, but the history of how Madras became popular in the west is one that is intriguing, and full of history.

Madras is still very popular today. Ralph Lauren is probably the most well associated brand to still use the fabric regularly. Many other brands have used Madras, brands from the high street, to the higher end, and those small independent labels in between. Every summer the lightweight and colourful plaid garments are in demand, and as I said at the beginning of this article, any sharp man of style should have a few Madras items in their wardrobe.

Seersucker – The Milk And Sugar Of Cool Fabric

The name seersucker is said to originate from the Persian words shîr and shakar, which translates to "milk and sugar". This most likely references the smooth and bumpy texture of the fabric, as well as revealing the origin and popularity of the fabric in the Middle East – just like the popularity of the Madras fabric during the British Colonial era.

Seersucker was a popular choice of fabric in countries such as

India, because the climate was warm and oppressive. However, it is also said that seersucker was used as early as the American Civil War, to make haversacks and more famously, the baggy trousers of the Confederate Zouaves, like that of the Louisiana Tigers. In addition to such clothing, the fabric was also used during the Victorian era for mattresses and pillowcases, becoming known as bed ticking. Seersucker proved to be a popular and more breathable and aerated fabric during the hot summers in the British colonies and in the southern states of America.

So, what is Seersucker? Obviously, it's a name given to a style of fabric – well – Seersucker is not just a fabric, the way it is woven gives it, its special and important characteristics. It is actually, a thin, puckered all-cotton fabric. It is commonly striped or checkered, and as already stated – it is most associated with summer wear and garments worn in warmer climates. It is most often seen in white and blue stripes, it can be found in other colours like yellow, pink or green, alternating with white stripes. It's often used for suits, shirts, shorts, dresses and robes, with its key benefit being its lightweight nature and breathability. If you have ever been up close and personal with seersucker, you'll notice that it is woven in such a way that some of the threads bunch together to give the fabric a wrinkled appearance. The advantage of this, is that less fabric is in touch with your skin, allowing space for air to move over your skin, allowing for a cooler feeling when worn. This also has another advantage. Seersucker is very quick and easy to dry when wet. Plus, it's wrinkled nature means it doesn't need ironing.

While Seersucker had been popular during the nineteenth century, it really gained its iconic status for its role in menswear during the twentieth century. Around 1909, New Orleans clothier Joseph Haspel Sr. began to make suits from seersucker which gained regional popularity due to their comfort and suitability for the aforementioned warmer weather. It is said that Haspel had been manufacturing workwear clothing for factory workers and felt that businessmen shouldn't have to suffer in hot offices, so he started a production run of seersucker suits at his New Orleans factory. Legend has it that while promoting his suits at a convention in Boca Raton, Florida, Haspel walked into the ocean up to his neck in his seersucker suit. He came out, hung the suit to dry that afternoon and then went ahead to wear it to the convention dinner that evening, looking both sharp, and smart.

Initially in the U.S. it was often poorer people who wore Seersucker, for the afore mentioned work clothes manufactured by the likes of Haspel. However, it was when preppy undergraduate students began wearing it in the 1920s in an air of reverse snobbery, that it really began to take off. Brooks Brothers was also one of the first companies to utilise the fabric, and naturally as the twentieth century progresses, so it's association with Ivy Style becomes more entrenched. Film stars, and musicians were seen to be choosing outfits using the fabric also. Notable wearers were Ivy Style icons like Anthony Perkins, Dustin Hoffman, Steve Mcqueen and James Coburn, and the jazz musician responsible for the Birth Of The Cool – Miles Davis. In the UK as we move into the sixties, the early Modernists and then the Mods who took style inspiration from Album covers, and movies began to emulate their musical and celluloid heroes by seeking out items or getting items made in the fabric. One familiar 1960s star who looked great in Seersucker was Brian Jones, who most likely came across the fabric when The Rolling Stones first went to the U.S.

Today, many brands still incorporate Seersucker in their summer collections, and over the years Seersucker has remained a popular summer fabric, and is just like Madras, a fabric for those who are style and comfort conscious – and therefore should have some in their wardrobe. I myself own a blazer, several shirts and some shorts. Without a doubt, such clothing keeps you cool... in more ways than one.

From The Correspondent — An Article About Brogues, Imperials And Spectators

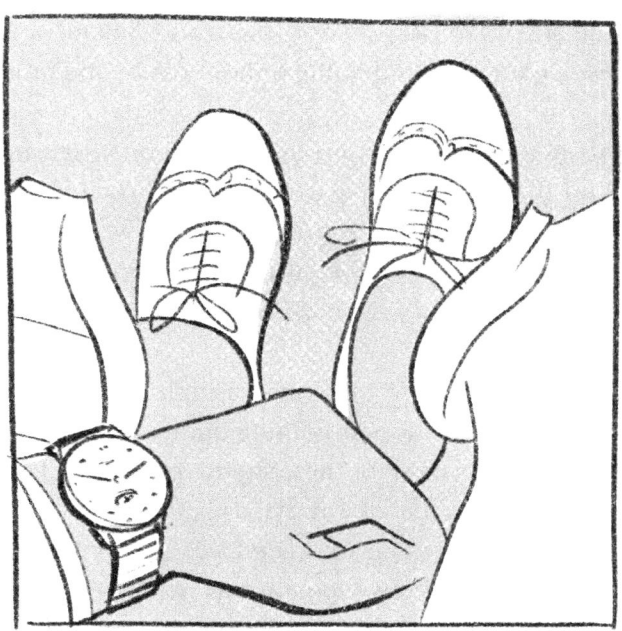

There are shoes that stand out, they look good, and do the job. Some are versatile and can be worn both casually and formally.

One such shoe is the Brogue. It's versatility has made it a fashion staple. But, not only that, it has helped spawn other styles that are associated with different aspects of life. Usually sport or leisure, rather than just for work, or the functionality they were originally created for.

The Brogue Shoe has changed quite considerably since it was first produced for farmers in Scotland and Ireland at the start of the 19th century, it was designed primarily for use outdoors and wearing in the countryside. It was pretty much a Farmer's shoe.

Brogues when they were initially manufactured were usually made in black leather, and were perforated in order to allow water from the boggy landscapes of Scotland and Ireland, to get out of the shoe, so, they could dry much more easily, and quicker.

During this period Brogues were never seen as smart shoes appropriate for the more upper-class business. Those upper classes when going to meetings or formal occasions, would not have thought of wearing such a shoe, as they were normally worn by the working classes. They were quite simply, just considered a working shoe.

In the 1920's the style grew increasingly elegant, with the Brogue element of the shoes becoming quite elaborate, and as a consequence a new market for these shoes opened up. They were soon to be seen on the feet of women, usually on outward-bound pursuits, as the shoe became associated with sports and sporting life. Its highest point of development was reached in the 1930's when the world's arbiter of fashion the Prince of Wales wore it as a bespoke golfing shoe made in suede with a grey lounge suit.

Thanks to two separate tones of the leather, these sportier shoes became known as Spectator's or Co-respondent shoes in the UK.

The reason for the UK term is in relation to English Law:

"Co-respondent in English practice, the alleged paramour of the spouse in a divorce action who is designated on the summons and served with the papers as well as the spouse."

King Edward VIII's relationship with a married American woman, Wallis Simpson, and their fondness for Spectator shoes, is no doubt the reason why they became known as Co-respondent shoes. The Kings abdication, and relationship with the divorcee was a real sensation across the globe, and it rocked the very fabric of English sensibility, duty and correctness at the time.

The two-tone leather brogue style was also favoured by the fashion conscious during the jazz era. Later, screen greats such as Fred Astaire and Gene Kelly wore the highbred brogues in many of their famous dance routines. Another variation on the theme was the saddle shoe. Originally created for adults and children in 1910 the modified brogue was made from white buckskin with a black or brown leather instep (hence the saddle).

By the 50's this style of shoe had been adopted by the newly liberated teenagers and was worn by both girls and boys. The former with bobby socks. The style became official when a young Elvis Presley appeared in the film 'Jailhouse Rock' wearing white buckskin saddle shoes.

But, jumping off the saddle, and getting back to Brogues, there are many great shoemakers and brands.

Famous manufacturers like Florsheim have continued to make brogues in various guises.

Florsheim's "Imperial" line of the mid-century cannot be improved upon by any modern shoe at any price in my mind, it seems to be the perfect shoe. Even the ordinary Florshiem's (non-Imperials) of the 80's and earlier, are an excellent single-soled shoe, similar in quality. But it is the Imperials Full Brogues, that have a massive, armoured heel, a double-sole Budapester with a storm welt, (technically, a "split-reverse-welt"), and the Florsheim Imperial Plain Front "Wholecut" Derby (Blucher) built on the same indestructible frame that are truly the standard-setters of the whole shoe industry.

These are better made than any ready-made shoe today and many bespoke, and well established brands – Including all the famous names, Lobb, Church, Crockett, Loake, Alden and so forth. These, in the best cases, may approach the Imperials, but never do they exceed them in terms of build or material quality. John Lobb ready-made are a great shoe for example, but somehow, do not achieve the same status and quality of Imperials.

Suggs, the Front man of Madness swears by them, as do many individuals who have an interest in the true quality of such heritage brands. In fact, in the UK, those that evolved out of the whole Mod and Skinhead scenes, and became Suedeheads, took to wearing Brogues, when they wanted to wear a more dressed up look. So, it isn't surprising Suggs likes them so much.

Both the Full Brogues and Plain Toe Derby's, in Scotch grain Calfskin and Shell Cordovan are quite possibly more supportive and comfortable, than most shoes, which is undoubtedly a godsend for a large or heavy man, or for any gentleman who happens to be on his feet all day. Florsheim's really do seem to be the brand that has achieved the benchmark that other shoes can only be compared to.

Getting back to the two tone styles of shoes:

Before the days of the spectator, it was the style — for many years — for men to wear spats. Spats were worn over the cuff of the shoe to accent the colour of the shoe and match the suit, while also protecting the wearer's calves and ankles from dust and dirt kicked up while walking. Because spats were relatively

The Desired Article

inexpensive compared to shoes, they allowed one pair of shoes to be worn with a wide variety of colours and patterns. When spats went out of style, the spectator came into style, leading some to believe that the spectator's colour design was an attempt to duplicate the look of spats worn over a black shoe.

Another theory is that the black toe and heel was intended to hide any grass stains incurred from walking, while maintaining the white summer dress shoes that were fashionable at the time. Specifically, these grass stains would be expected to be incurred by a spectator (the man, not the shoe) at the races or on the golf course.

Whichever, the truth is about the reasons for the two tone style of Spectators, the Spats idea, to me being the most plausible, the grass stain theory is just contrived enough to be a stroke of creativity that, I want to be true. It kind of adds to the romanticism of bygone times.

From Loafing Around To An Iconic Style: A History Of The Loafer

According to The Rake 'London shoemaker Wildsmith is credited with creating the first modern loafer in 1926 for client King George VI, in response to the stuttering regent's request for a bespoke casual shoe he could 'loaf' around his country houses in. A beefier ready-to-wear rendition suitable for outdoor use was soon put into production, and the style was quickly emulated by many more of Britain's gentlemen's shoemakers.'

Meanwhile over in Norway, there was other machinations afoot in the world of shoe making. Nils Gregoriusson Tveranger, had studied how to make shoes in the United States, and took inspiration from the moccasins that many of the indigenous native tribes wore.

The origins of moccasins go back to the cold, harsh climates of man's past that made it necessary to make protective footwear. Wearing moccasins or boots would have been essential to keep feet from freezing. In warm weather and mild surroundings, protective footwear would be less important, and people could easily go barefoot. The word moccasin, which has language origins with Eastern North American tribes, traditionally referred to a shoe with a puckered u-shaped 'vamp' over the instep. The name of the Great Lakes Ojibway tribe means 'people of the puckered moccasin'. The southern New England Narragansett word for shoe is 'Mocussinass' or 'Mockussinchass'. Today the word moccasin, still with innumerable spellings, generally refers to all types of hard and soft soled shoes, with and without puckered toes.

Worn by the hunters, fisherman and farmers of his fjord-side home in Aurland. The 'Aurland Moccasin' found favour throughout Europe in the 1930s, and visiting Americans brought the shoes home as souvenirs. Knowing a good thing when they saw it, Maine-based shoemaker GH Bass launched its version of Tveranger's shoe, named the Weejun in homage to its Norwegian origins, in 1934.

The Weejun is perhaps the most well-known loafer on the market. Many other companies have produced their own versions, some with greater success than others. The GH Bass Weejun however, has a history synonymous with style thanks to high profile style icons often wearing this stylish, comfortable shoe.

So, let's take a look at this particular shoe, and the different interpretations of it that have been produced.

The interesting thing about the Weejun, was that when the American company developed their Moccasin style shoe in 1936, not only did they put a firmer more durable sole on it. They put a supportive strap of leather across the upper with a diamond cut out. As the shoe became popular on American college and University campuses, so the slot in the strap became useful. It served as a place where they could slide a coin, should they need to keep money back for making either an emergency telephone call, or possibly to serve as a good luck charm. Hence, we today will still call such a style of loafer a 'Penny Loafer'.

A shiny penny made an attractive glint on the shoe, so when Italian designer brand Gucci made a foray into the loafer market producing their own versions of moccasins, so they added the decorative element of a snaffle. Which was inspired after a visit by Aldo Gucci to the United States. Mr. Gucci upon returning to Gucci's headquarters in Italy, set out to add a leather loafer to the house's list of products. The finishing touches affixed to each shoe's upper was a gold coloured horse bit, which was a staple Gucci symbol.

In the early 1950s shoemaker Alden, based in Massachusetts, created the tasselled loafer. This loafer style was perhaps considered slightly more elegant than the Penny Loafer as it was shaped with cleaner lines and a slightly higher and more sweeping profile on the foot, with the added decoration of the tassels. This enhancement has often been liked by dancers.

It is said part of the design on some tasselled loafers is taken from that of boat shoes. The lace goes around the shoe, through

The Desired Article

eyelets or tunnels before being tied off at the front with the tasselled end of the laces stopping them from loosening.

Other trappings and variations have been seen such as the Kiltie which was derived from Golfing shoes, a fringe of leather would hang over the laces say on a pair of Brogues, protecting them from mud on the golf course. Eventually this practical element began to adorn some loafers as decoration, although not for covering laces, therefore creating the fringed enhancement. Kiltie simply taking its name from the traditional Scottish form of dress. The Kilt.

Another prevalent addition to loafers was added by Sebago. This is termed as the 'Beef-Roll' The name is as it suggests. When a joint of beef is cooked the twine used to tie the meat, so as it keeps it shape whilst cooking is tied in a similar style to the way the reinforced stitching and extra thickness of leather at the seam each side of the instep is sewn. This addition gives the shoe more stability and longevity, as well as giving a more attractive look to the seam. Other brands have since adopted this innovative addition, purely because it strengthened the shoe.

Loafers as I have alluded too were extremely popular on Campuses, and this is not particularly surprising. After all, if you are in a rush to get to a class or lecture you didn't want to be wasting time fastening or undoing laces. The fact that loafers were a shoe you can easily slip on, meant they were practical. They soon became an Ivy Style staple, and icons of the American Ivy League Style of dressing such as John F Kennedy, would often be seen relaxing in such shoes. Likewise, another one of the style icons of the 20th century Cary Grant was a fan of the style. Other influencers include James Dean, Anthony Perkins etc. As well as musicians, such as Chet Baker, and later in the twentieth century and into the 21st many of the musicians that were part of the various Mod revivals. The most noted of course being Paul Weller. Especially when he formed The Style Council, after he called time on the Jam, when they were seemingly at the top of their game.

In fact, the style of loafers is such a classic style that it is often returned to by brands and will be seen in all their various forms. Originally a male shoe, they have also been adopted by women, and have become a traditional style for everyone. In the mid 20th century as we saw the evolution of the teenager, and in particular the modernist subculture, so we saw the adoption of the loafer by youngsters across Europe. The style was no longer confined to American colleges. The popularity spread pretty much worldwide. They are of course more considered as a shoe for dryer weather, and when it's warm, many people have been seen to wear them without socks. It may have originally been seen as a casual shoe, and indeed for very formal occasions a Gentleman is expected to wear a formal lace up shoe such as a Derby or Oxford, but in much more recent years, the classic nature of a loafer has made the shoe more accepted and can be seen worn quite formally. A well-polished Penny Loafer can look exquisite with the right outfit, as I am sure many style conscious Mods will attest to. With a nice flash of colour from a smart pair of socks, this style of shoe, can really add character to an outfit. There are many brands who produce loafers, and the majority of high end shoe makers will do these shoes as well. Also, the quality of leather can have a huge bearing on the price and artisanship of such shoes. Loafers made using Shell Cordovan, (considered to be one of the best quality shoe leathers), are highly sort after, and are popular for those who can afford the best.

The G H Bass Weejun though, is the original icon when it comes to this style. I swear by them. They're comfortable, and always look cool. Especially when I am just 'Loafing' around.

When It Rains, It Pours – The Return Of The Mac

You see them on the sharply dressed in movies, you see them on dishevelled Detective's, and they have become an enduring staple of the City Gent. Spies have worn them, as have Gangsters. I am of course talking about the raincoat. Or more specifically The Mac.

There are many great coat manufacturers that produce their own versions the world over. Brands such as Baracuta and Aquascutum for example. Now why is it known as a Mac, and how did this sort of coat come into being? You will no doubt have heard the coat referred to as a "Macintosh", and therein lies the obvious clue. For it was a Glaswegian chemist called Charles Macintosh, born in 1766, who was the son of a textile dye manufacturer, that after inheriting his father's business, made a discovery.

In 1823, he patented a process for bonding melted rubber to wool, which in turn, made the fabric waterproof. He founded the company Macintosh to sell his fabric to raincoat makers.

In the early years, Macintosh cloth was stiff, smelly, and prone to melting in the heat. Wool was not really the right fabric to use, but, considering the climate of Glasgow, it was presumably the first fabric you would think of.

The teething problems soon led to further inventive creations. Macintosh had been savvy enough to merge with the clothing company Thomas Hancock in 1830 and they began to produce their own ready-to-wear coats. Hancock had invented a method of vulcanizing rubber which solved much of the stiffness, smell, and melting problems. They had also had the foresight to use cotton instead of wool, whose oils tended to break down the rubber. They also learned how to tape and glue seams to resist the elements more than stitches alone. Consequently, the first of what would be seen as a modern raincoat was created.

Interestingly, the first intended use of the fabric that Macintosh created was for the use of waterproof tarpaulins for tents.

The Mac should not be confused with the Trench Coat, which was traditionally used Gabardine fabric.

The history of the trench coat actually starts almost 100 years before World War I. As amazing as this fabric that was used for the aforementioned Macs, which was for keeping the wearer dry and warm, they did have one major flaw – the fabric was not breathable, consequently, sweat was retained in the garment. As well as this, the fabric also had a rather unpleasant smell and could even "melt" in the heat of the sun, as already mentioned. Regardless of these shortcomings, The Macintosh were used throughout the 19th century by Army personnel.

So, who invented the trench coat?

Designers and fabric manufacturers continued to develop the material over the years, to try and make it more breathable, and more wearable. There are two clothiers who claim to have created the trench, and the arguments seem to continue. These two were John Emary, and Thomas Burberry.

In 1853, John Emary developed and patented a fabric that was just as water-repellent as the original rubberised cotton but was (thankfully) less smelly and more breathable. Emary renamed his company to what we now know as Aquascutum. This name comes from the Latin words "aqua" and "scutum" which translates to "water" and "shield." This name directly refers to Emary's focus on designing weather-proof clothing for the gentry.

It is said Emary created his version of the trench for officers serving in the Crimean War.

Thomas Burberry founded his business in 1856. Burberry is still one of the most recognisable labels rocking the fashion world. In 1879, the young draper invented "gabardine." This was a waterproof twill fabric that was also breathable. It was created by actually coating the individual yarns of cotton or wool. This was a big leap from the original fabric that was used to create the macs, where the entire piece of fabric was coated in one go. Burberry delivered plans for his new raincoat to the British War Office in 1901, where it was readily accepted.

Both Emary and Burberry's fabrics were very popular with

all types of gentlemen – from sporty types and explorers to the upper class and aviators. It is clear to see why these fabrics became an essential for military uniform. It is still unclear who truly invented the trench. Both companies had connections to the British military establishment, and both Emary and Burberry had previously developed weatherproof clothing similar to the trench.

The trench coat was designed to protect from wind and rain. They were not the warmest coats, however, they were supplied in a large size so that warmer coats and layers could be worn underneath them. In past wars, soldiers wore greatcoats. These were long overcoats of serge; a thick fabric made from wool. They were very heavy, long and cumbersome, despite being warm (when dry) In the trenches, the long greatcoats proved to be somewhat of a problem. They were very long and heavy, and would become weighed down with mud, making them even heavier. Soldiers found it difficult to use their equipment while wearing them. The trench coat was welcomed, as it was lighter, and it was much easier to move in it, and offered a great many uses, as well as being weatherproof and warm. In short; it was a very useful garment and much more than just a coat.

As stated at the beginning – the mac, and indeed the trench coat were seen regularly on our screens at the cinema, and of course on the television. Steve McQueen in Bullitt is a fine example, of a Detective wearing a mac. Michael Caine as Harry Palmer, a spy is another fine example, and then there is Alain Delon in Le Samourai who wears a Trench coat. Each of these stars of the big screen are veritable style icons. On the small screen, a typical detective wearing a Mac is Peter Falk in Columbo, his dishevelled look giving him a sort of disguise to his sharp and keen mind. Consequently, as Autumn arrives and the wetter weather that is

The Desired Article

to be expected, so the style conscious will search out those accoutrements that serve the purpose of keeping them both dry and warm. Trench Coats may seem to be seen less often, as they do seem less necessary. Their longer length not conducive to wearing whilst driving, but shorter Macs that come to just above the knee are more practical, and many retailers do still produce versions of these classic style coats, which are somewhat smarter than a military parka, or other form of hooded waterproof coat.

Falling For Flannel – That Autumnal Fabric, And Bags Of Style!

As soon autumn arrives, so thoughts start turning towards warmer clothing. There is a fabric that has been used for at least the last century that should be addressed, especially as it has seen a bit of a resurgence since certain period dramas on television (Peaky Blinders) for example have had an impact on tastes when it comes to tailoring. The obvious fabrics to write about are

Tweeds, and the use of different textures such as Herringbone, but these I will come to soon, but not yet. Instead, I will address a style that is truly classic. Because, if there was one outfit that defined British menswear during the mid-20th Century, it was the casual combination of grey flannel trousers worn with a darker contrasting sports jacket. For around thirty years, starting in the mid 1920s and then declining with the arrival of 'youth fashions' in the 1950s, this was the look that was seen everywhere. From the promenades and beaches of the seaside resorts, to the terraces of football stadiums and throughout society. This fashion crossed the boundaries of age and class. It was a look that was just as popular with the average British working man as it was among Hollywood's elite, (Fred Astaire was a huge fan of wearing Grey Flannels.) Even today, it is common to mix and match a jacket with contrasting trousers. Now when you hear the term flannel it conjures up a soft warm often woollen mixed fabric, and this is quite correct, but not exclusively so.

There are various types of flannel fabric — it is really a milling technique that can be used on a variety of textiles. However, to the majority, the focus is going to fall upon cotton flannel, normally used to make buttery-supple shirts, and woollen (or perhaps wool-cashmere) flannel, that is employed in suits, odd coats and trousers.

So, what is flannel, exactly?

Essentially, "flannel" simply refers to any cotton, wool, or synthetic fabric that fulfils a few basic criteria:

Softness: Fabric must be incredibly soft to be considered flannel.

Texture: Flannel has either a brushed or unbrushed texture, and both textures are equally iconic.

Material: While many materials can be used to make flannel,

not all materials are suitable for this fabric. Silk, for instance, is too fine to be made into flannel, which is supposed to be both soft and able to keep warmth in.

It's believed that the word "flannel" emerged in Wales, but we know for a fact that the term was in common usage in France in the form "flannelle" as early as the 17th century. While flannel was periodically popular among the French and other European peoples throughout the Enlightenment era, (the time of Rousseau, Spinoza and Voltaire) interest had waned elsewhere while Welsh flannel use managed to increase.

How is flannel produced?

First, the base material for flannel is acquired. Depending on the type of end product desired, this material would be cotton, wool, or a synthetic textile of some sort.

Next, the textile yarn is spun in much the same way that other fabric yarn is constructed. Some considerations may be made for yarn that's intended for use in flannel, but the main distinguishing marks of this fabric appear during the weaving stage.

A twill or plain weave is usually used to make flannel, and the woven fabric may be napped on one or both sides to create a soft texture that hides the weave. Napping is a process that distresses the spun fibres, and makes it take on the appearance of unspun fibre. Naturally, the fibre stays together since it has been woven into a matrix, but napping does decrease the durability of the fabric somewhat.

Synthetic flannel is often provided with a flame-retardant coating that may be toxic. Wool is naturally flame-resistant, and any number of treatments may be applied to cotton flannel. If you're looking for the safest, most organic flannel on the market, merino wool flannel is probably the wisest choice.

The Desired Article

Getting back to the traditional Flannel Suits of yesteryear you see examples in almost every classic movie of the mid 20th century. As stated, Fred Astaire liked wearing Flannel, when he wasn't dancing in top hat and tails. Gregory Peck actually starred in a movie from 1956 called The Man In the Grey Flannel Suit. Examples have been seen widely throughout history, and obviously movies have influenced and reflected styles of those periods.

Funnily enough when it comes to "Widely" seen examples, there is also a style of trouser that was quite popular in the 20s, and the 70s, and that was "Oxford Bags"

First, let's do a description. Oxford bags were typically made of flannel or another lightweight material. They are not particularly weird in terms of construction; a typical design sported all the normal pockets, had a crease down the front of each leg, and was cuffed at the ankle. Where things get weird is in their dimensions: these were among the earliest, perhaps the original, pants that were baggy to the point of ridiculousness. The most extreme examples could be 44 inches in circumference at the ankle; this is big enough to completely hide the lower leg and any evidence of a foot. For comparison, the leg opening of a Levi's 501 jean—a fairly loose cut, by modern standards—is 16 inches. These pants were bonkers.

The story of how Oxford bags became a trend is considered controversial; at least, as controversial as a debate over 100-year-old English trouser can create. The explanation for their size and name comes from 1924, at the University of Oxford, when the school administration supposedly banned the wearing of knickerbockers (or, more specifically, plus-fours). Knickerbockers are those baggy almost-pants that end at just below the knee. Plus-fours extend, as the name suggests, another four inches down.

(There are also plus-sixes and plus-eights.) Plus-fours were, the story says, beloved amongst students at the prestigious University. As a rebellion, the students decided to keep wearing them—but to wear something over them, to hide them. Something fairly lightweight and billowy enough to hide the already loose plus-fours they loved so dearly. And so was born a fashion trend. To me this sounds like an unlikely tale. There is also a more credible tale of rowers wearing wider leg pants over their rowing shorts. Much in the way a track suit is worn over an athlete's kit. The wider leg allowed them to put on and remove the said trousers without removing their shoes. Like anything, when things become popular there are those that try to push boundaries, and as a consequence the wider trousers became even wider and extreme.

Those fans of the style decided that if baggy was good, hugely baggy would be even better. The pants got bigger, and bigger. Twenty-four inches became, possibly as the result of a mix-up between circumference and diameter, 44 inches.

As the trend of huge trousers moved beyond Oxford—it moved to the U.S. very quickly and was rebranded and slightly retooled as "collegiate pants"—new parts of society began to realise that really baggy pants could actually be pretty useful.

Workers found that it was easier to move in looser pants, so discarded the wool flannel for hardier textiles like corduroy but kept the looser look. Criminals realised they could store all kinds of weapons alongside their legs.

The enormously wide-legged look fell out of fashion as quickly, as all extremes in fashion do, but it came back a few decades later. In the early 1970s, a new club trend started up in the cities of the north of England, spawning a movement which would come to be called Northern Soul. It was an unusual musical movement in that it didn't actually involve new music; instead, it was essentially a fan base of Northern English teens and twentysomethings with a passionate love of a particular brand of mid-1960s American soul. The music this scene favoured was generally the rarer and more up-tempo four to the floor music that was not initially commercial when it was first released.

The fashion for Northern Soul clubbers was just as specific and significantly older than the music they danced to: for men, it was, you guessed it, Oxford bags, paired usually with a tank top. But as with the likely original use of the Oxford bags, the Northern Soul kids liked Oxford bags because they were utilitarian: Northern Soul was very serious about its dance moves, which involved a lot of spinning and kicking the air and dropping down for splits.

Now we are in the 2020s the fashion world has been taking inspiration from some silhouettes from yesteryear and gradually we are seeing fabrics and styles returning and being adapted for modern times.

Weaving A Tale Of Tweed

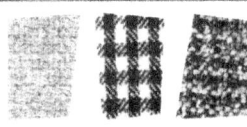

In recent years, Harris Tweed has achieved cult status having been rediscovered by the fashion industry.

Tweed is a wool patterned fabric that had become synonymous with Scottish and Irish style. The rough, twill fabric originated in the Scottish Highlands in the nineteenth century, and it is still used today for coats, jackets, suits, and many more items, including, accessories such as, hats, wallets, purses and luggage.

Tweed is an extremely warm, resilient fabric that is thick and stiff. Wool tweed is often woven using different coloured threads to achieve dynamic patterns and colours, most frequently with small squares or vertical lines. Tweed is particularly popular for tailoring and especially hard-wearing jackets, which were originally made using such material for hunting activities.

Tweed was originally called "tweel," which is the Scots word for twill, the most popular weaving technique for making tweed. The name, according to history, came about when a London merchant misinterpreted the name "tweel" for "tweed," thinking the fabric was named after the River Tweed in Scotland. The name soon stuck, and the fabric has been called tweed ever since.

The material that originated in Scotland and Ireland, was worn commonly by farmers. Tweed soon became popular with the upper classes across the British Isles after 1848, when Prince Albert purchased Balmoral Castle in Scotland and designed the unique Balmoral tweed. Each highland estate began to make their own "estate tweeds" to differentiate themselves during hunting expeditions and other such outdoor activities.

Tweed is, as stated, most popular for suiting and robust outerwear because a of its ability to keep in warmth and the rough and distinctive texture that makes it hard-wearing.

Tweed sports coats for hunting were one of the first uses of this fabric, and as with many successful enduring items, they have become traditional, and, because of quality, its popularity continues today.

Full tweed suits are quite popular also, especially in the last few years as popular television programmes and movies that are set in the early part of the twentieth century have helped reinvigorate the fashion industry and have had influence on the buying public. A full tweed suit can look extremely distinctive when accessorised well. It is without doubt a very classic look, and such history of the textile provide a great vintage appeal.

Tweed hats and bags are also a common use for the fabric. Tweed caps are characteristic of highland farmers and weavers and have become something of a fashion statement during the twenty-first century, as hats have also seen a resurgence in popularity after disappearing for a while.

There are said to be eight different types of Tweed, but this is open to debate.

There are many different ways to make tweed fabric, and the different types of tweed are named after the sheep they're made from, where the tweed is made, or after the type of weaving technique or pattern. Here are some of the most popular types of tweed:

Perhaps the most famous of these – is Harris Tweed: Harris tweed is a legally-protected type of tweed made in the Outer Hebrides, an archipelago off the northern coast of Scotland. According to the Harris Tweed Act of 1993, Harris tweed is strictly defined as:

"Handwoven by the islanders at their homes in the Outer Hebrides, finished in the Outer Hebrides, and made from pure virgin wool dyed and spun in the Outer Hebrides."

Donegal tweed: Donegal tweed is named for the Irish county

of Donegal, where it originated. This is one of the most popular types of tweed in the world, and it is distinguished by its rainbow-colored specks of yarn throughout the knobby surface.

Saxony tweed: Saxony tweed from merino sheep, originally made in Saxony, Germany. The tweed is very soft and smooth, due to the nature of merino wool.

Herringbone tweed: Herringbone is a form of tweed that is more about its distinctive pattern. It is a broken twill weave that produces a pattern of V's on the surface of the fabric. Some say the herringbone pattern looks like fish bones, hence the name.

Shetland tweed: Shetland tweed is named after the breed of sheep that originated in the Shetland Islands, a group of islands far off the north-eastern coast of Scotland. The wool is lighter and more delicate, creating a lighter weight, and more casual tweed.

Barleycorn tweed: The weave of a barleycorn tweed gives the effect and look of barleycorn kernels on the surface of the fabric. It's a very dynamic pattern and has a slightly bumpy feel.

Cheviot tweed: Cheviot tweed is named for the type of sheep used to make the wool, from the Cheviot Hills in the Scottish borders region. It is generally rougher and heavier than other types of tweed.

Overcheck twill: Overcheck twill is a plain twill fabric with a large checked design in a contrasting colour completing the tweed pattern.

It has to be noted twill is the weaving style used with tweed fabrics, and twill is not the actual fabric. Twill weaving can be applied to other fabrics.

Tweed was traditionally hand-woven on a loom. Today the entire process has been mechanised, but the process is largely the same.

First, raw wool is dyed and then dried in an industrial drier. These coloured wools are mixed together to make the exact shade of thread needed for a tweed. Each colour is weighed, roughly mixed by hand, and then blended in a giant industrial mixer to create the hue required for the pattern.

The mixed wool then goes through a process called teasing and carding, where it is drawn through a series of rollers covered in tiny spikes. This stretches the wool and makes sure the fibres are all pointing in the same direction so it can be made into thread.

Next, the wool is spun into thread and wound around yarns ready to be woven into tweed.

Tweed has been central to British style for centuries.

It comes in a variety of weights, weaves, and colours. This means there is no 'typical' tweed: the material ranges from plain and lightweight to colourful and heavy, covering everything in-between.

So – When was tweed invented? As stated, it became popular in 19th century. But tweed was invented in the 18th century initially by Scottish farmers to help them endure harsh winters.

During this time, tweed — which was known as Clò-Mór in Gaelic ('the big cloth') — was woven to be as weather-resistant as possible. It was extremely thick and didn't feature the colourful and intricate designs it is now renowned for.

The various Tweeds as we now know them were developed in the 1830s, when the British aristocracy took to the material. Its weather-resistant properties made it the fabric of choice for the staff uniform at their country estates, and the upper classes would commission unique estate tweeds that would blend in with the surroundings of their grounds.

In the 1840s, improved production methods made tweed more affordable. It became the fabric of choice for hunting and fishing clothing due to its weather-resistance, and the fact it helped the wearer camouflage into their environment.

Over the decades, as tweed production became more automated, it became affordable enough for those outside of the aristocracy. Today, it's a quintessentially British fabric that you can use to add sophisticated style to almost any outfit, and no man's wardrobe is complete without some sort of tweed. It's no wonder that it's strength and style has endured for such a long time, and it's use is still evident even in urban surroundings.

Corduroy: A Short History On The Fabric That Can Draw A Line Between — And Fashion

Corduroy, is it the marmite of fabrics? Some love it for its texture, and wearability. Some hate it because it is a fabric associated with the old fashioned stereotypical style of Geography teachers, pensioners, and those considered to be out of step geeks. Yet, every so often that Geek chic makes a resurgence, or the revival of practical workwear brings Corduroy back in the form of Trucker Jackets, trousers, and other examples of retro styles that were popular in other decades such as the 60s and 70s. Corduroy was even seen on football terraces during the mid 80s and early 90s thanks to brands such as Wrangler, Levi's and Lois. So, what is Corduroy's history?

Corduroy's roots are firmly rooted in the ancient Egyptian city of Al-Fustat. Located not far from the Nile River. The city became associated with its creation of tough woven fabrics sometime around the second century.

It also, at least for a while, played a very significant historic role—in 641, it became the first Arab settlement in Egypt and served as the country's capital for two separate periods totalling more than 300 years. But, in the midst of the Crusades, one of the city's top political officials ordered the city burned in a desperate attempt to prevent its wealth from being ransacked and stolen.

Since that time, Al-Fustat lost its high level of influence in the region, as nearby Cairo, which was only founded in 969 AD, took its place in the 12th century, and became Egypt's new capital.

Getting back to Al-Fustat – it turned out, that this lost city's biggest legacy in the Western world was the predecessor of fabric that was to become known as corduroy, this original fabric became known as fustian, a clear riff on the Egyptian city's name. It was a heavy cloth that worked well for garments such as trousers, but unlike corduroy, it doesn't feature any raised cords

Fustian, of which the two known types we have today are velveteen and corduroy, were originally woven with a warp of linen thread and a weft of thick cotton, so twilled and cut that it showed on one side a thick but low pile.

So, why and how did this Fustian material become known as Corduroy?

It was originally believed that the term corduroy came from a 17th century English corruption of the French "corde du roi" or "cloth of the king," this theory however has since been debunked. It is believed that the term is a compound of the word "cord," referring to its tufted, row-like pattern (or Wales), and "duroy" which was a coarse woollen fabric used in England. What we now recognise as corduroy emerged in the late 18th century in Manchester, England as factory wear during the all-important Industrial Revolution. It would remain a working class fabric for the next hundred years, only to be discovered in the 1960s by college students and beatniks alike who wore it as an alternative to their chinos and denim jeans. By the late 1970s to 1980s, the popularity of corduroy trousers, and even shorts grew among preps and surfers—only to be re-appropriated in the US by flannel-clad rockers during the grunge era of the 1990s.

In the UK, as brit pop took hold you would see corduroy trousers paired with a tracksuit top and a pair of trainers. A look that was both considered comfortable and cool by those that had moved away from more formal attire as club wear became practical when going out at the weekend. An outfit I myself would sometimes wear. I had a pair of Lois Jeans jumbo cords in navy that I particularly liked. These teamed with a pair of Gazelles, and an Adidas zip top, in Manchester in the late 80s early 90s was not an uncommon sight amongst teenagers at the time. The appropriation of comfortable clothing was in very much the same way as soul fans had dressed more for comfort whilst dancing in the 70s.

As we reach the noughties, Corduroy all but disappeared from the high street, but was still available from smaller and more specialist outfitters. Usually adopted by those that hankered for vintage style. Now, in 2020 cord is available more easily on the High Street, as new generations warm to the often autumnal shades that Cord is often available in, and the trends of the past are revisited, and the possibilities of the fabric are applied to many things, other than just clothing.

There is another weave similar to Corduroy known as Bedford. So, what is the difference between Bedford Cord and Corduroy?

Bedford cord is a fabric weave with ribs down the length of the fabric, similar in style to Corduroy. The ribs can be any width. It looks like an uncut un-brushed corduroy but does not have that softer and more comfortable velvet feeling.

Bedford Cord gets its name from the town of Bedford, in England. It is a very strong and durable fabric, it is often used in upholstery and for work clothes. The Bedford Cord is usually a combination of two kinds of Weave, namely "Plain" and "Drill"; however, others may be used.

Weft floats decide the width of the cords on the back, and wadding ends may be used to emphasise the prominence of the cords.

Personally, I prefer Corduroy to its harsher "cousin". For example, an Ivy Style soft shouldered jacket in corduroy is always smart when teamed with the right clothing.

The Origins Of Paisley, Ancient Babylon, And Indulgence

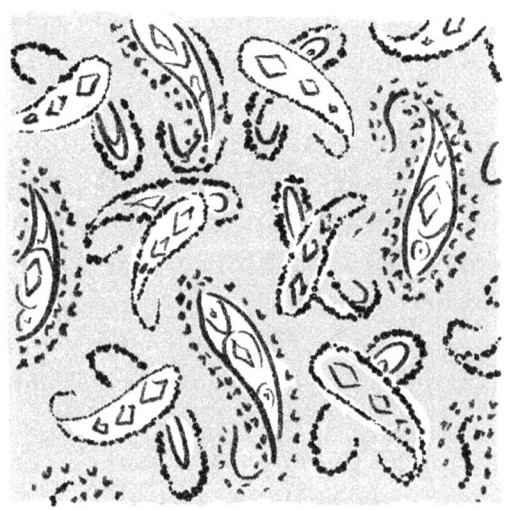

Although it was originally called buta or boteh, meaning "flower," People have seen resemblances to lotus flowers, a mango, a leech, a yin and yang, a dragon, and a cypress pine.

In ancient Babylon, it was likened to an uncurling date palm shoot. Providing them with food, wine, wood, paper, hatch, and string—those things that people need—date palms symbolised prosperity and plenty. Paisley began its life as the privilege of cosseted, powerful men. It was considered to be extravagant, and somewhat self-indulgent.

According to Jude Stewart in Patternalia: An Unconventional History of Polka Dots, Stripes, Plaid, Camouflage, & Other Graphic Patterns.

Kashmiri shawls sprang up as early as the 11th century but found their first promoter in Zain-ul-Abidin, who ruled Kashmir from 1459 to 1470 and encouraged weavers from Persia and Central Asia to move to his kingdom. Their next champion was Akbar (reigned 1556–1605), who made the shawls central to the Kashmiri practice of khil'at, "robes of honor" ceremonially exchanged in political and religious contexts to establish a clear pecking order. (Being on the receiving end made one submissive and therefore inferior to the giver—not awesome, although scoring the sumptuous textiles made for luxurious compensation.) Shawls given as khil'at were decorated with all sorts of patterns, although some scholars wonder if the paisley motif came to predominate because it resembled jigha, a crown insignia jewel used to pin a feather to a courtier's turban. (Gradually the jigha elongated, more and more resembling the feather it anchored. So, yet another reading: Paisley is a feather.)

Shawls started infiltrating Europe in the late 18th century, when Kashmiri princes began including British East India Co. Officers in their ritual shawl-giving. The English officers sent the shawls home to their sweethearts, who clamoured for more. Fresh from conquering Egypt and next sniffing around India, many of Napoleon's officers found themselves stationed near Kashmir and similarly tempted by the shawls. Napoleon's wife Joséphine began stockpiling paisleys, and by the early 1800s, European desire for paisley had intensified into a frenzy.

Textile manufacturers noted paisley's popularity, and that it could be profited on, and the race was soon on to produce more shawls. Importing finished shawls from Kashmir didn't come close to meeting European demand, so it wasn't long before manufacturers scrambled to produce their own. In Norwich, England, and Edinburgh, Scotland, factories soon thrummed to life, cranking out worthy imitations, although no amount of tinkering with silk, cotton, and wool blends could compete with the original pashmina wool for softness. A Kashmiri monopoly made the raw material impractical to import, so textile manufacturers shifted their focus to gaining other advantages: accelerating production time, lowering manufacturing costs (and retail price), and blitzing consumers with more dazzlingly complex designs.

Skip forward a few decades and in the 1960s we see great changes in Britain and Europe. Commonwealth immigration saw the Asian population of Britain grow, and as the decade moved culturally towards its looser more liberated, 'swinging' period thanks to post war children coming of age. Fashion and music began to reflect a generic cosmic influence, epitomised by the Beatles' time with the Maharishi Mahesh Yogi in India in 1968. Hippiedom was taking over from the much more tailored button up look of Mods just a few years before. The world was opening itself to everyone with travel and television, and music. Different cultures were influencing fashion, and as a consequence Paisley became hugely popular once more. Paisley also echoed the psychedelic period where thought and lifestyles were being challenged thanks to the psychedelic properties of LSD. The trip on acid made colours seem brighter, or more complex, and the hectic yet somehow ordered swirls of pattern that made up Paisley helped reflect the experience. I could go on about how Paisley became more accepted by the mainstream. You only need to look at some ties from the 80s that reflect this. As businessmen added a bit of flair to their Conservative suits with a tie, that had such a pattern on it. Towards the end of the 80s, it wasn't quite as predominant as it had been.

In the 90s however, when the psychedelic drug Ecstasy appeared, there was a period when Paisley became popular again as a new "Swirley" psychedelic taste in music and fashion became popular. Nightclubs were become Mecca's for Ravers, and retro fashions became popular again in some style tribes. On the independent music scene bands like Kula Shaker, and Oasis even took a leaf out of the precedent set by the Beatles in the late sixties and used influences from the Sixties, and subsequently India in their music, and as a consequence this new psychedelic period gave rise to Paisley being popular again. When Liam Gallagher ex lead singer of Oasis started his own brand Pretty Green, it was natural that he would use Paisley in many of the brands collections.

Paisley may disappear from time to time, but it is never far away, as its popularity and possibilities are endless.

It is as pleasing to the eye now to some, as it was in ancient Babylon, and will no doubt remain inspiring artists and fashion designers for a long time yet.

Conclusion

To conclude this book which saw the bringing together of the articles I have written about these clothes and fabrics, I feel it is only right to refer to perhaps someone who's own book on mens fashion was an integral part to my education when it comes to style. That is of course Hardy Amies, whose own book, the ***ABC of Men's Fashion (1964)*** helped steer me to an even better understanding. Already interested in clothing and style I purchased this book by off chance while in Manchester, when I was still a young man. It served as an interesting read to someone who had found himself working in Menswear for the high Street giant Next. Before 1982, Next was known as Hepworths and they were renowned for over a century, between 1884 and 1985. Hepworth's had been a thriving national chain of men's clothing shops, with a strong line in ready-made and made-to-measure suits. Rivals in the same field included Montague Burton, and The Fifty Shilling Tailor (later renamed John Collier). They managed, much like Burtons to supply men with the clothing the British public required. Hardy Amies did actually help design some of the suits Hepworths would produce, and when in 1982, Hepworths decided to rebrand and modernise – so Next was created, and has gone on to be one of the highstreet leaders in a time when retail has been going through a lot of upheaval and change. Whether you like Next or not, and prefer the more exclusive clothes available from designers and artisans, rather than the mass-produced clothing, Next is known for– it has to be said that without the likes of Burtons, Hepworths et al – the clothing industry for the masses would have really struggled. Many young men would not have been able to achieve a sense of style that was affordable across the nation.

Working for Next, I have seen many styles come and go – and things evolve in a way that shows that these Google fried times are changing the way we shop. However, in my mind true style needs that classic shopping experience. The seeing of clothes that have been finely crafted by innovative artisans, and people who understand the practicality of a product. I hope in some small way, what I have shared in this book helps to establish a connection with great pieces from our past, so in a true modernist ideal, they can be taken forward, and instead of dumbing down, and producing with inferior quality – find those innovations to improve and sustain that legacy of great menswear for the discerning gentleman, who knows true style when he sees it. I have said it before, Style is timeless, and fashion comes and goes quickly. This book I hope will preserve some style at least – and will indeed be of interest for a long time. After all it is a history book of those articles of clothing many desire.

JD.

Afterword

'Jason Disley understands desire, he like many of us lusts after the cool things, the perfect collar roll, the finest merino knit and that elusive sack jacket that is out there but you just haven't found it yet, but he also has that other obsessive quality that men of a certain age or type possess, an unforgiving curiosity to know every single detail behind the garment, its heritage practicality and enduring popularity, this book fills you with that sheer enthusiasm safe in the knowledge that your chosen penny loafer or preferred Harrington jacket irrelevant of its price or brand comes from a place that once we enter we can never leave, though the book is centred around the mid century modernist Ivy League preppy style staples Jason takes us further back to discover the roots of real modernist styling and shows its progression to today's modern menswear, informative fascinating and essential'

Paul Stafford, Spring 2022.

Acknowledgements

There could quite possibly be a never-ending roll call of those who have helped, encouraged or inspired this book. From movie stars, to musicians, to friends who have felt I should write a book about those things I deem as stylish. More known for poetry and fiction this book is a departure from what I have written before. What follows is a list of some people I wish to acknowledge, people who have directly or indirectly inspired my passion for sartorial discovery. No doubt I will have missed some names and will wish that I had added them after this book goes to print. For this I can only apologise in advance.

Firstly, I must thank my wife Shirley Disley, who puts up with my obsessions.

Matteo Sedazzari and Zani for believing in me.

Mark Head for his wonderful design work and illustrations.

Mark Baxter for his contribution, inspiration and encouragement.

Paul Stafford for his comments at the end of this book.

Gary Byrne for asking me to provide some content for Modernist Influence.

Gary Malby at Gama Clothing, a man whose tastes overlap with my own, and digs my creativity.

Rick Blackman for the confirmation of an idea I was toying with. He voiced it and gave me the courage to go ahead and make it happen. This book may never have happened if it hadn't been for his message to turn my articles into this very book.

John Simons, no reason needed.

Claudio De Rossi, a constant inspiration, whose style and knowledge is vast, and beautiful.

Claire Mahoney, Chris Davies and Graham Lentz at Detail magazine.

Other people who I wish to acknowledge are:

Hardy Amies, Cary Grant, Steve McQueen, Anthony Perkins, Steve Marriott, JFK, the fictional character James Bond, Fred Astaire, Miles Davis, Chet Baker, Paul Weller, etc, all of whom have inspired my tastes in stylish attire.

The following is a list of those that have either inspired my writing, or have supported my work in some way.

Nick Keen, Alf Button, Andy Kennedy, Jason Brummell, Tony Beesley, Jason Joules, Graham Marsh, Barrie Sharpe, Rafael Diez Rivera Boluda, Ciarán Peppard, Kai Ahland, Memo Torfilli, Robert Garnham, Becky Nuttall, Mark Hynds, Adam Cooper.

Steve Margrain, Ash Raddon, Steve Cradock, Andy Crofts.

Richard Cooke (for the encouragement during Lockdown).

Mark Powell, Martin Freeman, Alex Banks, Marley Faria, Neil Sheasby, Neil Jones and Stone Foundation, who provided the soundtrack while I was writing. Ian Pople, David Alexander, Charles Caine Shirts. Lorenzo Salvatori at Capirari. Ian Moore, Eddie Piller, Ian Longman, Stuart Deabill, and Tom Hoy.

Lastly, I wish to thank *you* for purchasing, and reading this book
Jason Disley, Summer, 2022.

PERFORMERS

Irvine Welsh and Dean Cavanagh revisit the dying days of the 1960s to reimagine what happened during the making of the first true British cult film.

They Don't Think They're Gonna Let You Stay in the Film Business.

Performers deals with masculinity at the point when the sexual revolution was saturating culture. For many working-class men, it was confusing and threatening. As secularism started to replace traditional Judaeo-Christian attitudes, a lot of men found themselves torn between embracing the liberation and clinging to the simpler, more morally binary past.

In the swinging and hallucinogenic London of 1968, visionary Scottish filmmaker Donald Cammell joined forces with cinematographer Nicolas Roeg to make "Performance". The film would star James Fox, Mick Jagger, and Anita Pallenberg, but the casting process was frustrating for Cammell because he insisted on bringing "real villains" into the roles that supported the lead character of South London gangster Chas Devlin.

What Welsh and Cavanagh identify is that strange cultural moment in 1960's London when bohemian intelligentsia flirted with the world of organised crime

VARIETY

Book One of ZANI's Tales Trilogy

A CRAFTY CIGARETTE
TALES OF A TEENAGE MOD

Foreword by John Cooper Clarke.
'I couldn't put it down because I couldn't put it down.'

'Crafty Cigarette, all things Mod and a dash of anarchy. Want to remember what it was like to be young and angry? Buy this book. A great read.'
Phil Davis (Actor Chalky in Quadrophenia)

'A Great Debut That Deals With The Joys and Pains of Growing Up.'
Irvine Welsh

'A coming of age story, 'A Crafty Cigarette' maybe Matteo Sedazzari's debut novel but it's an impressive story.'
Vive Le Rock

'It's a good book and an easy read. That's pretty much what most pulp fiction needs to be.'
Mod Culture

'A work of genius.'
Alan McGee (Creation Records)

'Like a good Paul Weller concert the novel leaves you wanting more. I'll be very interested in reading whatever Matteo Sedazzari writes next.'
Louder Than War

A mischievous youth prone to naughtiness, he takes to mod like a moth to a flame, which in turn gives him a voice, confidence and a fresh new outlook towards life, his family, his school friends, girls and the world in general. Growing up in Sunbury-on-Thames where he finds life rather dull and hard to make friends, he moves across the river with his family to Walton-on-Thames in 1979, the year of the Mod Revival, where to his delight he finds many other Mods his age and older, and slowly but surely he starts to become accepted...."

A Crafty Cigarette is the powerful story of a teenager coming of age in the 70s as seen through his eyes, who on the cusp of adulthood, discovers a band that is new to him, which leads him into becoming a Mod.

ISBN-13 : 978-1526203564

Book Two of ZANI's Tales Trilogy

THE MAGNIFICENT SIX IN TALES OF AGGRO

Foreword by Drummer Steve White (The Style Council, Paul Weller, Trio Valore,)
'A vivid and enjoyable slice of London life in the 80s, with a wealth of detail and characters,'

'Tales of Aggro has got the feel of 'Green Street' and a touch of 'Lock Stock and Two Smoking Barrels'. This is fiction for realists.'
Vive Le Rock

'A real slice of life told in the vernacular of the streets'
Irvine Welsh

'Laugh out loud funny, exciting and above all, written with real warmth and passion for London and the Character's making their way through this tale and life itself.'
Gents of London

'It's A Treat to Read, Just Like A Crafty Cigarette'
John Cooper Clarke

'Tales of Aggro is lively and funny'
Phil Davis (British Actor - Quadrophenia, Silk, The Firm)

'Tales of Aggro is a kind of time machine that takes one back to the days of 'Scrubbers', 'Scum' and 'Get Carter'. Very redolent of those atmospherics.'
Jonathan Holloway – Theatre Director and Playwright

Meet Oscar De Paul, Eddie the Casual, Dino, Quicksilver, Jamie Joe and Honest Ron, collectively known around the streets of West London as The Magnificent Six. This gang of working-class lovable rogues have claimed Shepherds Bush and White City as their playground and are not going to let anyone spoil the fun.

Meet Stephanie, a wannabe pop star who is determined to knock spots off the Spice Girls, with her girl group. Above all though, meet West London and hear the stories of ordinary people getting up to extraordinary adventures.

Please note that Tales of Aggro is a work of fiction.

ISBN-13 : 978-1527235823

TALES FROM THE FOXES OF FOXHAM

Fictional fantasy fun, with a sprinkling of Harry Potter and Star Wars ethics to add to the aura.
Scootering Magazine

A wonderfully original story that certainly appealed to me and my daughter, who loved it.
Our Favourite Shelf: Mod & Beyond in Print

'A lesson on understanding, empathy, inclusion, and expectancy.
Mods Of Your Generation

A magical adventure story set in the 1950s that transports the reader to the bustle of Naples, the thrills of London, and the tranquillity of Norfolk. As the reader encounters quick-witted and cheeky foxes, Vespa riding wolves, stylish bears, reliable badgers, good & bad witches on the way, in a host of exciting situations, resulting in a dramatic battle of good versus evil.

Out Now on Amazon

MORE BOOKS FROM ZANI
www.zani.co.uk

Feltham Made Me – Paolo Sedazzari
Foreword by Mark Savage (Grange Hill)

The poet Richard F. Burton likened the truth to a large mirror, shattered into millions upon millions of pieces. Each of us owns a piece of that mirror, believing our one piece to be the whole truth. But you only get to see the whole truth when we put all the pieces together. This is the concept behind Feltham Made Me. It is the story of three lads growing up together in the suburbs of London, put together from the transcripts of many hours of interview.

ISBN-13 : 978-1527210608

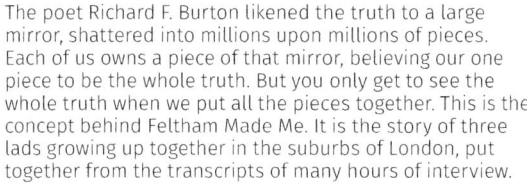

The Secret Life Of The Novel: Faking Your Death is Illegal, Faking Your Life is Celebrated - Dean Cavanagh

"A unique metaphysical noir that reads like a map to the subconscious." **Irvine Welsh**

A militant atheist Scientist working at the CERN laboratory in Switzerland tries to make the flesh into Word whilst a Scotland Yard Detective is sent to Ibiza to investigate a ritual mass murder that never took place. Time is shown to be fragmenting before our very eyes as Unreliable Narrators, Homicidal Wannabe Authors, Metaphysical Tricksters & Lost Souls haunt the near life experiences of an Ampersand who is trying to collect memories to finish a novel nobody will ever read. Goat Killers, Apocalyptic Pirate Radio DJ's, Dead Pop Stars, Social Engineers and Cartoon Characters populate a twilight landscape that may or may not exist depending on who's narrating at the time.

ISBN-13 : 978-1527201538

7P'S Paperback – A.G.R

The 7 P's. An unusual title you may think, but its meaning will become as apparent to you as it did for four friends and comrades who, in a desperate move of self-preservation, escaped the troubles of 1980s Northern Ireland, and their hometown of Belfast, only to find themselves just as deep, if not deeper, in trouble of a different kind on the treacherous streets of London.

ISBN-13 : 978-1527258365

ZANI ON SOCIAL MEDIA

After enjoying *Tales from The Foxes of Foxham*, please follow ZANI on Social Media.

ZANI is a passionate and quirky entertaining online magazine covering contemporary, counter and popular culture.

Follow ZANI on Twitter
twitter.com/ZANIEzine

Follow ZANI on FaceBook
www.facebook.com/zanionline?fref=ts

Follow ZANI on Instagram
www.instagram.com/zanionline/

Printed in Great Britain
by Amazon